C000150660

A SIGNIFICANT YEAR

THE ARAB LIST

ABDALLAH SAAF

A SIGNIFICANT YEAR

EDITED AND TRANSLATED BY
DAVID ALVAREZ

LONDON NEW YORK CALCUTTA

SERIES EDITOR
Hosam Aboul-Ela

SEAGULL BOOKS, 2019

Original © Abdallah Saaf, 2008

First published in English by Seagull Books, 2019
English translation and notes © David Alvarez, 2019

ISBN 978 0 85742 543 0

British Library Cataloguing-in-Publication Data
A catalogue record for this book is available
from the British Library

Typeset by Manasij Dutta, Seagull Books, Calcutta, India
Printed and bound by Hyam Enterprises, Calcutta, India

CONTENTS

TRANSLATOR'S
FOREWORD

Professor of political science at the University of Rabat, former cabinet minister, leading voice in civil society and veteran observer of the Moroccan political scene, Abdallah Saaf has authored books on subjects as varied as the Gulf Crisis of 1991, the sociology of knowledge in Morocco and the democratic transition in his country.

A Significant Year (*Une année considérable*) is in part a sociological and political report on the state of the Moroccan nation on the eve of the 2007 general elections, a crucial moment in the years following King Hassan II's reign (1961–99). But in its descriptions of the author's car trips across large swathes of his country between June and September of the title's eponymous year, the book also borrows from the road-movie genre.

Part travelogue, part sociological analysis and part political prognosis, *A Significant Year* can also be situated in a longue durée continuum of Moroccan and other Arab travel narratives that reach at least as far back as the twelfth-century *Rihla* (*Journey*) of Ibn Jubayr (the classical model for the genre of travel writing in Arabic), and whose most celebrated exponent was the Tangiers jurist, Ibn Battuta, who travelled extensively throughout the fourteenth-century Muslim world and beyond, and who wrote vividly about the locales he passed through or in which he lingered and about the people he met there.

However, rather than focus on the customs and affairs of other peoples and places after the manner of his illustrious forerunners, for the most part this exceptionally well-informed Rabati narrator trains his steady if roving gaze on his own country. Saaf's overriding concern is to get a good feel of how the Moroccan people have been faring since the accession of Mohammed VI to the throne, a period during which they have been caught up in a dizzying dialectic of deep continuities and jagged discontinuities, all of which the author situates within the context of larger and longer patterns of structurally uneven and unequal development.

In undertaking a symptomatic reading of his country's condition at a turning point in its national unfolding, Saaf also continues the ongoing project of decolonizing the production of knowledge about Morocco to which he and such figures as Abdelkabir Khatibi (one of his interlocutors during the road-trip) have made such notable contributions. Despite the deceptive simplicity of its narrative structure, *A Significant Year* gives us a nuanced rendition of the multiple intersecting, clashing and often mutating perspectives and interests that configure the country's social and political formations.

In reading this text, we see this complex nation-state not through the frequently exoticizing and therefore simplifying gaze of 'outside' onlookers but through the inexhaustibly curious eyes of a seasoned observer and indefatigable local traveller who is deeply attuned to the international dimensions of the country's colonial and precolonial past as well as to the globalized aspects of its current circumstances.

The elections that prompted Saaf's purposive excursions took place forty-one years after Morocco's independence from France and Spain, so that the book is not just a report on the state of the nation a few years into the new monarchy but also an account of how the country has fared since it shook off colonial rule. Ranging from the dizzying heights of the Rif and Middle Atlas to the sand-swept desert roads of the Western Sahara, from the small resorts of Morocco's Mediterranean coast to the large urban centres of the country's middle belt, and alighting at many other points in-between, Saaf's text is also a kind of unwitting tribute to his country that in an utterly unassuming manner makes palpable the depth and range of the author's own dogged commitment to its betterment.

Most of the people and customs that Ibn Battuta describes in his narrative are only of abiding interest to specialists, and yet centuries later all of us can read the globe-trotting jurist's account of his travels with pleasure. Similarly, for all the many contemporaneous acronyms, political parties and topical figures that Saaf invokes, his text partakes of some of those qualities that have lent Ibn Battuta's *Rihla* such enduring interest, including the narrative's close attention to the intricacies of a variety of life-worlds and locales, and a companionable style that combines colloquial discussion with erudite disquisition.

But perhaps the most salient feature of *A Significant Year* is the way in which it testifies to its author's unremitting probing of the seeming given-ness of the world. In peering closely at its surfaces, Saaf repeatedly plumbs its depths. Thanks to the intensity of the author's looking, the reader's knowledge is also widened and deepened. In the end, we feel as if we have been riding along in the passenger seat of Saaf's small Peugeot, participating in his peripatetic search for meaning all the while.

ABBREVIATIONS

CCDH: Conseil Consultatif des Droits de l'Homme. (Former name of Le Conseil national des droits de l'Homme.) The Kingdom of Morocco's National Human Rights Council, a government human rights organization.

CDT: Confédération Démocratique du Travail. (The Democratic Confederation of Labour) A Moroccan national trade union centre.

IRCAM: Institut Royal de la Culture Amazigh. (The Royal Institute of Amazigh Culture.) A government-sponsored centre for the promotion and diffusion of Amazigh (Berber) culture, founded by royal decree in 2001.

OADP: L'Organisation de l'action démocratique populaire. A left-wing party founded in 1983 that eventually merged with other parties and political groups to form le Parti socialiste unifié (the United Socialist Party), a secular left-wing party.

PADS: Parti d'avant-garde Démocratique et Socialiste. (The Socialist Democratic Vanguard Party.) A left-wing political party founded in 1989.

PJD: Parti de la Justice et du Développement. (The Justice and Development Party.) A conservative Islamist democratic party., which has led the executive branch since November 2011.

PPS: Parti du Progrès et du Socialisme. (The Party of Progress and Socialism.) Formerly, the Moroccan Communist Party. After the fall of the Berlin Wall, the party adopted a socialist platform.

RME: Marocains Résidant à l'Etranger. (Moroccans Residing Abroad.) An official designation for members of the Moroccan diaspora, estimated to number more than four million.

RNI: Rassemblement National des Indépendents. (National Assembly of Independents.) A centre-right party, affiliated with the Liberal International.

UMT: Union Marocaine du Travail. (Moroccan Labour Union.) The oldest Moroccan labour federation.

USFP: L'Union Socialiste des Force Populaires. (The Socialist Union of Popular Forces.) A social-democratic party, founded in 1975.

SONASID: Société Nationale de Sidérurgie. National Steel Company. The largest steel company in Morocco, heavily involved in the construction industry, and partly owned by King Mohammed VI's holding company.

TRANSLATOR'S NOTE

The text presented here was written in the run-up to Morocco's 2007 parliamentary elections and then published in 2008 as the main part of a book whose long final chapter consisted chiefly of a highly detailed assessment of the electoral results and their ramifications. Since that assessment is primarily of interest to specialists, and since the original version of it is in any case available on the website of the think tank that Professor Saaf directs, with his consent I have chosen not to include the bulk of it in this English-language version. I have, however, included the assessment's first few paragraphs which here appear under the guise of the Epilogue.

On a related note, I have omitted parts of Chapter 9 that delve into the details of the hustings, and thereby rendered that chapter analogous in length to most of the others.

Finally, in the interests of greater readability, I have condensed the Preface and the first three chapters of the 2008 book—all four of which chiefly address questions of methodology—into a compact Prologue.

TRANSLATOR'S
ACKNOWLEDGEMENTS

The translator would like to thank Dr Hosam Aboul-Ela for the opportunity to translate Dr Abdallah Saaf's work and for his advice. He would also like to thank Dr Saaf for his courteous and helpful responses to various queries.

PROLOGUE
—
WHY A ROAD-TRIP?

A road-trip is an indispensable way of getting to know one's country better, of feeling its pulse. Investigating the most pertinent items for a report on the current state of the nation—whatever use one might want to make of such a report—entails visiting the country's regions regularly so as to rummage around in them, ferret out useful information and discover what's really going on.

In writing about national issues, I wanted as much as possible to have in mind the peasants of the Gharb region, the people of the Rif, the fishermen of Larache and of Tan Tan, the civil servants of Rabat or of Marrakech, the mineworkers of Ouarzazate, of Youssoufia, of Boucrad, the artisans of Fez, the agricultural workers of the Zaer region or of Tadla or elsewhere . . . In listening to them, in learning about their lives, I wanted to shed the peremptory arrogance of those of us in the centre who think we have all the answers.

Concomitantly, I wanted to conceptualize the country and the links that bind it by continuously travelling between the different points that make up its territory. We are what we are by virtue of our relations with others, and a journey is a key way to apprehend, analyse, interpret and comprehend the heart of a matter. It's also a useful means for letting go of convictions that have been acquired far too readily and that may be wide of the mark.

One doesn't have to crisscross the entire country to observe that, while there are several Moroccos—often in the very same place—at the end of the day, and as an abundance of evidence makes clear, it's a single country we're talking about. In any case, I was really in the mood to get on the road and, right away, these trips turned out to be decisive. What they've amounted to isn't just an effort to get out of the capital in order to take the measure (insofar as it's possible to do so) of how things are really going in the heartland and the rest of the country. Rather, my trips have also been inspired by a desire to visit the nation's regions, to listen to people, to multiply the angles of approach, to see things from closer up, to give my interlocutors a chance to respond to the way I see things and to reflect on what they themselves have seen and heard.

The point is to observe the country, to try and wrest some truths from its current conjuncture by taking advantage of the prevailing atmosphere during the days that separate us from the elections, and then, later, during the elections themselves and their immediate aftermath. At the same time, I don't mean to make of the elections a more decisive event than they can actually be. Often, we're guilty of subscribing to a worldview that deems elections a key to unlocking the mystery of the universe. That said, the 2007 elections, like their forerunners in 2002, are far from being the ordinary affair that they might seem to be on the surface. There's nothing banal about holding a popular vote.

Be all that as it may, I'll proceed by painting a picture of the country on the basis of notes I'll be taking during my travels with a view to grasping and assessing the changes that have taken place across the land. At a deeper level, I want to lift the veil that clings to reality and go straight to the heart of things, which the comfort of our convictions and our fixed ideas often distances us from. Through these interior journeys, it's our individual and collective selves that I seek to encounter and delve into.

Where to travel? What sites to visit? What parts of the journey should one highlight? Why select certain places, villages, towns and regions, but rule out others? Why return to some of them several times? The itinerary I've chosen, the sample of places I present, could easily be confused with a list of Morocco's main summer resorts. It includes large cities and some of the country's most significant tourist sites, e.g. Nador, Al-Hoceima, Tangiers, Tetouan, Kenitra, Rabat, Casablanca, Marrakech, Agadir, Laayoune, Smara, Dakhla . . .

But the most representative and significant places are not usually to be found where one might think. Sometimes, towns marginalized by politicians or simply by the ordinary evolution of things (e.g. Guercif, Rommani, Larache . . .), or even a neighbourhood, a boulevard, a street or an alleyway can be much more significant than an entire city. I won't be citing a good number of places that I'll have duly visited in accordance with the project's requirements, since to do so would entail reproducing things I've seen and said elsewhere. To be sure, the places I haven't included in this journey aren't devoid of interest. And it's in any case vital to keep asking oneself

3

what it's advisable to look at and highlight during this trip as well as with whom to discuss the trip's purpose.

I conclude this prologue by noting that I intend to undertake this journey in a dialectical sort of way, in the sense given to the word 'dialectic' by currents of classical thought associated with Aristotle, among others. Such an approach dictates that, in order to carry out an investigation of the truth, several actors must observe a great variety of places and themes from various angles. This Aristotelian procedure pits itself against monologues or solitary discourses. The sort of intimate discussion that, for instance, Marcel Proust carries out in his description of Madame de Guermantes shows how the subject of *Swann's Way*[1] has multiple facets that are difficult to grasp from a single vantage point, which is why Proust undertook to approach them from a variety of standpoints. It's not by chance that solitary approaches to knowledge often lead to considerable disappointments. In contrast, the polyphonic and contextual 'dialectic' in question here entails several ways of seeing and deploys a plurality of perspectives in order to decipher reality. It allows for arguments for and against that can't but enrich our understanding of the subject. The truth, therefore, can only come from visiting different corners of the country.

1.
RABAT:
THE AGDAL QUARTER

Rabat. End of June. I've been spending time in the Agdal quarter ever since my undergraduate days and I'm still very attached to it. In a cafe which I've been frequenting for years—it's true that coffee-shop culture was less developed back then than it is today—I remark several things.

First, directly across from where I'm sitting, people are busy getting ready for the grand opening of a shop that carries a sign which ostentatiously reads 'Vineyards of Numidia' in Roman script.[2] The notion of opening a shop that specializes in local wines strikes me as rather bold. Given the current climate—we're living at a time of radical religious convictions, of terrorism, and of an insane violence that's as unpredictable as it is unexpected—the idea strikes me as rash, indeed, as suicidal. If Islamism, fundamentalist or not, is as strong as has been said during recent electoral campaigns, how can it allow such things to happen? Can the Morocco I see here, which on a day-to-day basis seems to so closely resemble the old Morocco, really have undergone such a transformation? Lately, the press has been reporting on emergent cultures, not just among the young but also amid all social strata: new behaviours, new ways of thinking, of being and living that are increasingly different from the old ways, a new spirituality, a new sexuality . . . Should one conclude from all this that a great new diversity has come into being? And incidentally, why call the shop 'Numidia'? If it were up to me, I'd dub it 'The Vineyards of Mauritania Tingitana'![3]

Second, like everybody else, I've just heard a rather surprising communiqué on the radio: the Ministry of the Interior declares that it has in its possession information from 'reliable' sources according to which politically motivated acts of violence—acts that these days are dubbed 'terrorist'—are going to be carried out somewhere in the country. In the past, this sort of information was systematically kept under wraps. Has the new transparency been gaining ground? Could a calendar of electoral activities really have been deliberately set up against a backdrop of terrorist threats?

At any rate, with every passing day, an entire discourse of contradictory images has been enveloping the land, and it isn't just spread by the media. I count among my friends a good number of journalists who work for the 'independent' press, and I always get the impression that they cast their coverage of the country in a rather sombre and negative light. They're accused of being systematically contrarian, of being nihilistic, of not seeing the good things that are being done wherever they're being done, of becoming the champions of no change, and of thus allying themselves in objective terms with conservatives. Doubtless, one can sometimes reproach certain texts with focusing on the spectacular, and even of performing a kind of violence on how we understand the country's reality by indulging in hyperbole and made-up stories. There's no doubt in my mind that the tendency to present Moroccan affairs as negatively as possible has become an obligatory posture for all respectable intellectuals. It's the new political correctness.

On that note, a friend of mine, who these days is one of the country's most visible journalists, painted a dark picture for me of the general political situation, in particular of the decision to cut back on civil service staff by encouraging 'Voluntary Retirement'. Apparently, the makeshift measure has had disastrous consequences for good governance. Among other things, in letting go of people it's let go of experience and expertise, and weakened, diminished and depleted such strategic sectors as health, education and administration ...

Contrariwise, officials with whom I've crossed paths lately (which, ever since I decided to respectfully keep my distance from all things institutional and official, has happened purely by chance) paint a totally different picture, and provide glowing reports on the smooth progress the current reforms are allegedly making. On my way back home from a brief trip to Asia, while I'm waiting for a connecting flight in Paris, I run into one of the ministers in charge of economic and financial affairs, an old colleague of mine at uni. After we greet each other, I listen attentively to his assessment of the state of the nation. Subsequently, for the flight's entire two-and-a-half-hour duration, I'm treated to a veritable press briefing, to a campaign in favour of the public policies currently being pursued. My interlocutor's evaluation of the ensemble of actions undertaken by the government he serves and of its decision to implement a 'Voluntary Departure' policy is positive and indeed enthusiastic.

Whom to believe?

At the end of that same day, I come across another journalist, the editor-in-chief of a French-language weekly that's very much in vogue, who also outlines his worldview to me. There's a battle being waged across the entire country between two die-hard camps: the forces of democracy and the forces of change. In his view, his task as a journalist is to contribute to the creation of true democracy. Along with his publication, he positions himself as a militant for modernity. I'm no longer quite so sure that journalists should work under this sort of banner . . . Nowadays, many dubious activities appear to find refuge in this sort of journalism: for instance, journalists now routinely lecture activists from parties that used to be regarded as the dominant actors in the political arena. These days, journalists seem to regard themselves as the new political experts. What's more, culture in its consumerist guise has also set up shop in the press, in the form of whole pages given over to ads for cars, fridges, homes . . . for all the useable goods you can imagine, in the models and colours of the most uniformly globalized designs imaginable . . .

2.
—
RABAT

July, Rabat. At the start of this summer, I learn the terrible
news that political scientist Alain Roussillon, director for
many years of the Jacques Berque Centre,[4] has died after suc-
cumbing to a violent cerebral haemorrhage. With Alain's
death, I lose a friend and an intellectual partner of exceptional
calibre. I've seen him at work as a political analyst and as a
researcher, I've listened to him on many occasions, and I've
read and reread a good number of his texts, nearly all of them,
in fact. The occasions when we communicated with each other
and discussed and debated assorted matters are uncountable,
so important was it for each of us to engage the other. Alain
Roussillon was a man of analysis, of synthesis, a practitioner
of intercultural exchange, an observer of the real, an inter-
preter and theorist of facts and of social tendencies, forceful,
subtle, open, stimulating.

He's left us written proof of all of this. Moreover, certain
pages he wrote are inscribed in my memory. I incline especially towards the exchanges that were so essential for both
of us. We co-authored numerous pieces, worked together on
various texts, notably in translating them from Arab to
French and vice versa, drew up research projects and colloquia
and exchanged arguments. Somewhere, I describe him as a
specialist in 'reformology', in past and present reforms. But

he was above all an intellectual devoted to research, attentive to social change, to a variety of discourses and to the positions assumed by key actors in the situations that he studied.

One day he left his post at Rabat, and at once I felt the absence of his intellectual companionship. Afterwards, from 2002 onwards, I saw him in Cairo every time I travelled there. In March 2007, during a visit to that city, he invited me to have supper in what he regarded as one of the last storied restaurants associated with the Arab Enlightenment, one of the few that hadn't gone down the path of re-traditionalization followed by such establishments as the famous Groppi.[5] Surrounded by portraits of the great figures of the nineteenth- and twentieth-century Arab Nahda(s)[6] in thought and in arts and letters, we spoke at length about the ongoing social transformations taking place in Cairo today. He spoke to me for a long time about the city's neighbourhoods, its suburbs, its Islamists, its town planning, its crime, its social outcasts . . .

He assured me that class contradictions were even more pronounced in Egypt than in Morocco and the worlds of poverty even harder to interpret, as were the unheard-of practices of subcontracting the State's operations. He saw Egypt as the favoured testing ground for the re-deployment of India-style globalization, with its proliferation of products, merchandise and cultural behaviours. Throughout our conversation, I once again savoured Alain's particular way of reading diverse facts as paradigmatic symptoms of current social phenomena. For instance, for a long time we discussed a dramatic incident which these days is almost regarded as a banal occurrence on the streets of Cairo: thirty-odd abandoned children had been killed by a gang of older youths. This indefatigable 'reformologist' was an untiring reader of the region's political, economic, social and cultural realities.

I saw Alain again two months ago at the CEDEJ, the centre he directed in the Egyptian capital. He offered me copies of his latest writings, or at least of the ones I didn't yet have. We parted after having planned numerous activities for the near future. One of them was his participation in the summer school organized every year by the Centre for Studies and Research in the Social Sciences (the CERSS),[7] which this year was to take place in Tetouan-Martil in mid-July. Days before it was scheduled to begin, Alain excused himself for not being able to participate.

3.

RABAT—MEKNES—FEZ

End of July, Meknes. There are two sorts of questions the elections raise. They may seem to contradict each other but in reality they're complementary. The first is: What's the place of the upcoming elections in the lives, activities and preoccupations of ordinary people? I don't just mean the people of Rabat, Casablanca and other big cities, but also those who live in the quieter parts of the country, who are surrounded by and wrapped up in the consensus and who are sometimes referred to as 'the silent majority'?

The other is: What can the elections deliver to the country? And how might the current state of the nation (in political, economic and social terms) influence an event that's as necessarily significant as the elections of September 2007? At the risk of repeating myself, I should point out once more that I'm not solely concerned with the election as such or with its purely political consequences. Rather, I'm especially interested in discerning how to take advantage of the present moment to better grasp the country's deepest realities.

Apropos of the timing of the elections, there's a detail that I find intriguing. This is the first time that the state has organized elections in the summertime. In the past, they've sometimes taken place in June or September. However, they've never been scheduled for the high season. Might the decision to hold elections right after the end of the summer holidays be some sort of trick for bringing about a certain desired result? Or is the choice of September 2007 tied to other reasons?

Perhaps the vote's been scheduled for September 2007 in order to prioritize regularity, at all costs, in the timing of election cycles. It's logical to think that elections should be held at regular intervals and that this timing should play a vital function in the construction of a democratic regime.

But September 2007 may also have been chosen with other ends in mind than forming a government according to the institutional calendar that the constitution stipulates so as to ensure that all the relevant institutions can get to work by October. Achieving this goal is symbolically important; nonetheless, I don't think it's a determining factor. The ultimate aim is to inaugurate a new political period by ensuring the renewal of the elites via the replacement of whoever needs to be replaced.

On that note, it's good not to exaggerate the place of Parliament in the order of things. In Morocco, the Parliament isn't endowed with sufficient powers, and in the final analysis parliamentarians are really no more than para-political actors. I asked a deputy in the outgoing legislature why he wasn't running for Parliament in September. I was astonished to learn that this legalistic gentleman, who couldn't be more of a monarchist, had decided not to run for office in his usual ward which is located in the heart of the Rif. 'Because,' he replied, 'given the overall equilibrium in the distribution of forces in Morocco, the power allotted to parliamentarians is too limited. Until now, my constituents have been quite willing to elect me to office, because they still have a fair bit of respect for my family and me, but if I insist that I get voted into office, they'll stop electing me.'

Until recently, a good number of decision-makers and voters experienced the elections as both a potential means for defusing social tensions and as an indicator of the ills that eat away at the body politic. They were regarded as an occasion when the country gets its breath back, tries to dispel its collective halitosis, unveils its hidden faces, and tries to secure uncertain liberties.

In any case, the choice of September 2007 really does seem problematic. The elections are imminent, and yet it's still unclear what people really think, what they're proposing, what debates they'd like to see and what it is that they want from the politicians. No clues about the public's thinking can be gleaned from the unpredictable agricultural cycle, or from the general air of dissatisfaction across the country, or from the middle classes, despite their many frustrations.

It's pretty clear that the notion that the current power structure is going to be reset, rebooted and reprogrammed, and that new programmes and platforms are going to have to confront one another in the public arena, in short, the notion that the upcoming national elections will constitute a democratic turning point is, at least for now, a vision of the distant future.

Leaving the capital on this 30th July, I decide to start my trip by driving over to the eastern part of the country.

On this occasion, Meknes is merely a staging post on my trip to Fez. Starting from Lahdim Square,[8] I go on my ritual tour of this city. First, a tour around the medina. This is my umpteenth visit to the Palace of Pasha El Jamii, and I still find the city walls imposing. The atmosphere here is of a kind I've only ever experienced in one other place: Beijing's Forbidden City. I also visit Al Mansur Palace, the former sultan's summer residence which these days is home to a cultural association. Meknes, with its ex-colonial districts, its middle-class living quarters, its suburbs ... Unsurprisingly, this city's political class is quite close to that of Rabat which is only a two-hour train ride away. Meknes is also home to a significant intellectual community that participates quite readily in national debates without appearing to be unduly impelled by local concerns.

From the outset, the elections don't seem to have assumed a visible and palpable presence in the life of the country. Everyone can observe that this is the case. For instance, anyone driving to Fez can see that at no step of the way are there any signs that a ballot is soon going to take place.

In driving up to Fez, I'm engaging neither in cultural tourism nor in academic fieldwork. Instead, I'm gleaning on-the-spot impressions, and probing feelings and states of mind that strike me as significant, even as I bear in mind that appearances can be deceiving. In any case, this is the guiding principle underlying the research trip that I'm beginning on this very day: to produce a kind of travel narrative-cum-reportage which, by focusing on its everyday life, delves into the state of the nation at a specific moment in its transformation.

At the down-at-heel luxury hotel where I decide to settle in for the night before venturing any farther, the season is low, as the tourism industry likes to say, but the prices are high, without, as far as I can tell, there being any justification for it. In any case, it's here that I decide to spend the night. This one-night stay marks my exit from the country's official centre and from the circle of those who think that they're in the know and who feel no need to travel anywhere to see what realities on the ground are like.

Fez represents many things at once: the more-or-less well-maintained relics of a proud past; the developments always taking place in the city centre, the science and technology park under construction. The popular and the aristocratic, the vulgar and the refined, relations between the 'well-born' and the working classes . . . there's no doubt about it—we're in a spiritual, historical, political and intellectual capital city that's long served as a commercial hub channelling off and redistributing the surrounding region's agricultural surplus.

Property in Fez is of an exclusive character. The control that Fez exerts over its hinterland is one sign of this. Its inhabitants (Fassis) own numerous gardens and orchards in the city's immediate surroundings. Land acquisition has tended towards the concentration of property, and both the weakening of the peasantry and the concomitant rural exodus have been going on since the colonial period. Much has been written about the significant development of Fassi capital, but I wonder whether current developments have made it lose its old character.

Fez also expresses the spiritual character of its economic life by means of its *habous*,[9] the lands that it's opened up for cultivation, and their extensions. At the same time, the city has not managed to curtail social exclusion and poverty. The traditional bourgeoisie has benefited from new sources of wealth. Furthermore, over the course of recent decades, the arrival in force of the liberal professions, of high-ranking civil servants, of military officers and of other agents of the State has changed the order of things.

Both property in the Fez region and what is referred to as 'Fassi capitalism' are built on a robust process of 'melkization',[10] large properties, high concentration of property ownership, important migratory fluxes, sustained urban growth, the extension of the built environment, and certain demographic facts.

Fez has undergone continuous transformation. On the whole, the movement of migrants from the interior to the city has been considerable, and the built environment has extended deep into the hinterland. There's a marked housing shortage in large areas around the city proper and growth has centred on the surroundings. The old city seems both to have extended its boundaries and to be deserted. For some time now, urban families, along with new waves of migrants from the countryside, have been settling at the city's perimeter. Property speculation has also taken over the entire periphery. Concretely, this speculation takes the form of satellite agglomerations around Fez: shantytown belts, new peripheral districts, urban centres situated farther away (some of which, like Ras El Ma and Ain Chkef, date from the colonial period), small roadside agglomerations with embryonic populations (Tnine Mhaya) . . .

Several highly varied kinds of locality have bloomed and been increasingly integrated into the city or its immediate suburbs (Zouagha, Ben Souda, Aouinat Elhajjaj, Montfleuri, Sahrij Gnawa . . .), several different fields of economic activity determine the life of the city, notably agriculture and the many agro-industrial factories, the railway and its ramifications, the development of cereal production, a significant commercial sector, financial and social services, military sites such as Ain Cheggag.

It's visibly the case that electoral activity only seems to interest narrow elite circles. The fielding of candidates is taking place on the quiet.

I drive around. The more I crisscross the city and its environs, the more improbable it seems that serious candidates haven't yet begun to undertake the necessary groundwork in their wards. Just a few weeks away from the start of the electoral campaign, they appear to be doing nothing.

4.
FROM FEZ TO THE RIF:
GUERCIF, NADOR,
AREKMANE

31st July.

I set out from Fez, and leave behind the factory smokestacks at the city's southernmost end. These dark stains on the natural landscape are like lesions caused by some incurable illness. You've got to drive for several kilometres out of town to shake off the oppressive image of these dismal blotches that occupy earth and sky. The black smoke that the chimneys incessantly belch up is proof that the city suffers from a serious sickness.

In the foothills of the Rif, one begins to enter another country. I remember maps illustrating the locations of the Rif's tribes. The region's tribal structure constitutes a kind of hidden geography, invisible but crucial. Aspects of an analysis of the Rif War[11] come back to me, the theory of tribal zones formulated by Jean-Paul Charnay.[12] Apparently, the zones played a key role in the the war and influenced both the conduct of the guerrillas and the manner in which the latter were repressed. At first, when Abd el-Krim and his men waged war in the vast spaces where their tribes held sway, they were strong and combative and often emerged victorious from battles. Moved by a powerful *esprit de corps*, they seemed indomitable so long as they remained within their domains. However, the farther they moved from their tribal territories, the more their force waned and the more vulnerable to defeat they became.

On the road, the sight of successive roadblocks manned by the police or by the gendarmes gives the impression that the country is in a state of alert. But neither the searches nor surveillance seem very thorough. In comparison with Lebanese checkpoints, ours seem purely routine. In any case, a terrorist would have to be foolish to drive along the main roads or to enter or leave a city via the official entry and exit points where security posts are set up.

Guercif hasn't changed in years. It's had little chance of doing so. Perhaps the coast can undergo changes, but can the hinterland? It remains stuck within its own timeframe, which almost corresponds to that of nature itself.

The signposts indicate that the city of Oran—inaccessible via the road I'm travelling on—is 447 km away. I know that the road that leads to Oran really does exist, but the destination seems imaginary.[13] A mischievous highway goblin insists on giving the same directions about the same destination at the end of the road I'm driving along. Oran, which is situated at Algeria's westernmost end, really could lie at the terminus of this road, if, that is, the frontier between Morocco and its neighbour had not been closed for decades.[14] The road-signs on the outskirts of Nador also indicate the distance that separates it from Melilla, a city occupied by the Spaniards,[15] just like Oran once was, but much more accessible than its counterpart.

On this 1st August, the sun is blazing over Nador. Perhaps all power must return to the people, but for the time being the people are on holiday. They are sunbathing on the city's beaches. Has the Rif's historic isolation finally been broken by this road that abruptly forks just a few metres from the entrance to Taourirt? Or is it due to the new coastal road, at least, the bits of it that have thus far been built along the Mediterranean littoral? The new road is relatively drivable in comparison with the old roads which were extremely dangerous, even deadly. Until very recently, the old coastal route was highly uneven; as for the new roadway, it hasn't yet appeared on maps.

I now enter a part of the country which I've frequently visited before. Over the past few years I've often come here on one mission or another, sometimes on holiday, at other times to attend a conference or a seminar. I've consulted a large number of books and documents on the region. Two years ago, I brought my students here in order to undertake a diagnostic assessment of the territory and I prepared myself thoroughly for our field visits. While here, we gathered a lot of information and read and heard a lot about the region as a whole. Moreover, afterwards, the students from that MA programme wrote dozens of reports and monographs about our site visits.

In my briefcase, I've got factsheets on Nador's industries that refer to a mining company (Seferif) which is in the process of winding up. The factsheet also contains information about Seferif's subsidiary, Marost, which exports the best of the local catch in fish and shellfish. This range of economic activities makes Seferif a major employer and redistributor of revenue in the region. Numerous businesses of all sizes have seen the light of day as a result of Seferif's involvement here: agricultural, food, textile, construction, fertilizer, mechanical, metallurgical, electrical . . .

I should perhaps be referring here to an 'eastern' region. I think that these zones are still in gestation, and that they're characterized by a relatively lively economic and social activity. One notes a greater tendency towards industrialization rather than commerce in the suburbs of Nador, a city which has in effect become an industrial centre.

In the projects undertaken by local and regional entrepreneurs, one can readily observe signs of their status as emigrants. International migration is a major player in local activities. According to some researchers, one of the first waves of such activity was linked to the economic situation of colonial Algeria. Afterwards, migrants from the Rif descended upon Morocco's interior in response to seasonal demand. Later, they migrated to Germany, the Netherlands, Belgium and other European countries. Migration has become a permanent feature of Riffian life, and guarantees the area a significant influx of revenue. Moroccan migrants abroad have become an economic force. At this point, about half of all Riffians live in foreign parts.

I knew that Nador was an important financial centre, given the enormous quantities of money deposited in the vaults of the impressive number of banks registered there. The city has long ranked among the top places for making deposits in Morocco. Virtually all of the country's banks are represented there. Analysts delight in stigmatizing this unusual concentration of banks and deposits, as well as the fact that the banks don't make significant efforts to share the wealth with the local population.

From early on, state policy was oriented towards heavy investments in the steel industry and infrastructure. The SONASID company took the shape of an imposing integrated industrial complex devoted to the transformation of local or regional raw materials. In both its regional and its international activities, the firm has embodied the will of the State. These days, I often hear it said that SONASID is essentially 'a simple rolling mill that transforms imported plain steel into coiled iron bars . . . ' Nevertheless, thanks to this industrial complex there's a certain dynamism in the air. The company sells its products to local businesses and there's no doubt that the signs of a substantial process of mature industrialization have multiplied.

At the start of the 1970s, the State decided to equip Nador with a truly modern port. With the arrival of the rolling mills, the creation of the port took on even greater significance. Nowadays, with the quantity of steel that it exports from its wharves, the port of Nador is one of the most important in the country.

No picture of Nador's economy is complete without mention of contraband- and drug-trafficking which are at once ubiquitous and invisible. Mention must also be made of the service industries and commercial activity. All the signs suggest that there's considerable continuity between legal commerce and the black market.

In the evening, the TV reports that the sordid saga of the twenty-three South Koreans kidnapped by radical elements of the Iraqi insurrection is getting bogged down in the muck.

The news is just in: the poor fellows have been decapitated. I think that responsibility for their deaths also lies with whoever sent them to that country. There's no doubt about it: the occupation of Iraq is becoming nightmarish.

Nador, 2nd August.

Wherever I go, I notice that service is lacking. Whether you eat out cheaply or at an expensive restaurant, the hygiene is always unpredictable. Ultimately, the picture I'd been given of Nador and its environs as a summer paradise has little to do with the reality I encounter wherever I turn.

On another note, the city thrives on its Amazigh culture and identity, the revival of which takes on specific characteristics in different regions. H.K. is a young man from the area with whom I get together during the activities of the community association to which he belongs. I have a lot of time for him. He tells me about local struggles over the cultural and linguistic issues that the Amazigh revival raises and introduces me to what would otherwise be an impenetrable world. These days, Amazigh claims are more forceful than ever and Amazigh identity reflects the equilibrium of forces that must serve as the basis for negotiation . . . Numerous community associations are organizing around issues such as greater autonomy for the Rif region. Essentially, they seem to be advocating a federalist option for Morocco . . . I have no choice but to acknowledge the significance of the autonomist movement. At the end of the day, however, it's marginal in relation to what's at stake in the region's establishment politics. Behind the scenes, political elites devote themselves to pre-electoral manoeuvres in which Amazigh identity plays no role.

I reflect on the different positions that it's possible to adopt vis-à-vis the elections. Along with some friends with whom I communicate by phone every day, I'm beginning to assume the role of electoral observer. 'But being an electoral observer is a way of avoiding having to take part in elections,' I'm told by a friend in whom I confide my intention to observe the legislative elections in my capacity as a community-organization official.

Driving around Nador, I observe on shopfronts a name that's been widely adopted by the town's residents: Illias Ice Cream, Illias Hairdresser, Illias Butchers, Illias this and that. Thanks to the toponymy of storefront designs, Illias, a common name in the Rif, contributes to the construction of a regional identity.

On this morning of 3rd August, I drive in the direction of Arekmane, some 25 km from Nador. I find a beautiful beach: fresh water, clean sand, and no sign of the elections on the beach or in its surroundings.

I relax on the strand, and in fact give myself over to a whole day of relaxation. The signs inform me that there are attendants at this beach; in other words, this isn't a wild strip of coastline. However, food options at this resort are unpredictable, the hygiene is questionable and services are pretty shoddy. When it was decided that China was going to host the Olympic Games, the Chinese proceeded to train all those workers who were going to come into contact with foreigners. They were brought up to scratch with regard to daily comportment, and, most notably, with regard to healthy lifestyles, to the aesthetics of social settings and to the arts of service. Fifty years after independence, we Moroccans should pay more attention to manners and civility . . .

A beautiful beach with lovely water, as lovely as any of the beaches of the north, and clean to boot, less polluted than the beaches of the north-west coast (Tangiers, Tetouan). Nevertheless, customer care is appalling. Every time you eat out at Arekmane, you risk getting food poisoning. The resort's flies form clouds whose thickness is as uncommon as their peskiness.

The way in which the gendarmes question people certainly doesn't make them come across as humble. In fact, it's entirely reasonable to deem their behaviour rude, arrogant and uncouth. They're always intent on flaunting their power, even over people who are typically submissive and ready not just to compromise but also to go along with police corruption by handing over bribes; in other words, people who seem quite capable of handling these small doses of excessive power. The end of the Years of Lead[16] seems to have had no discernible effect on this situation.

I head down to the hotel's terrace to have a coffee and read. Before long I'm approached by acquaintances from the local Amazigh movement, and an impromptu meeting with the organizers of a colloquium on regional autonomy takes place. They talk to me about their well-known gathering and invite me to take part in it. Since I can't really speak about an issue that I haven't had the chance to reflect upon adequately, I make my apologies.

It's clear that these magnificent coastal spaces can fulfil an important function as seaside resorts and as places of recreation. The presence of emigrant families who have come here from Kebdana[17] is an unmistakable sign of that. This is an important element of the new generation of facilities that are giving the greater Nador area a new character.

As for the upcoming elections, here as elsewhere there are few visible signs in public spaces that they're about to take place.

5.

THE RIF CONTINUED:
THE MOUNTAINS, AL HOCEIMA
AND SAÂÏDIA

On 4th August, I head out in the direction of Al Hoceima, at the heart of the historic central and western Rif and structurally isolated and systematically cut off from the rest of the country. As soon as one crosses a certain line, a frontier that's been traced out by nature, this part of the Rif takes on particular characteristics. One feels a strong sense of being in a space whose self-enclosed quality is the result of the various natural and social forces that have shaped it. The physical causes of the region's isolation are plain to see. One can clearly see how this region of mid-sized mountains plunges sharply into the Mediterranean. Furthermore, in travelling back and forth across the Rif, one becomes aware that its configuration comprises and is shaped by three distinct zones.

From Jebel Tisirene to Jebel Tidighin (2,456 metres tall) and beyond, the region is of a robustly mountainous character. The traveller can readily appreciate why the Rif has suffered from problems of communication and transportation. Geographers avail themselves of jargon to explain the zone's fragility, and point to its composite character and to the existence of 'geomorphic elements dating back to the Palaeozoic'.

I had assumed that the danger of falling rocks was merely theoretical, but various examples I see make clear that it's real enough. What's more, in this month of August, all the *wadis*,[18] which are usually short-lived and fast, are without exception entirely dried up.

The more one travels around and observes the region, the more readily apparent another zone becomes: a coastal belt that stretches to El Jabha, in which the Bokkoya massif gives rise to a magnificent landscape of forest-covered sierras that sometimes attain heights of over 2,000 metres. Like the first, this second zone is also visible to the naked eye.

In the course of several trips, one can also make out a third space. This one consists of the central zone of the mountainous region which is continental in character. It forms dense and compact groups of mountains which increase in size towards the south-east and contain basins amid the heights, depressions and deep valleys ...

The approach to Al Hoceima passes through imposing massifs that encircle the town. Whatever route one takes to get to the city, one notices that around these parts the Mediterranean coast is narrow and towered over by mountains, and that the uneven and craggy coastline places serious limits on maritime activity. Various channels of water give onto the sea and form little bits of beach. Hoceima is the only true bay in the area.

These geographical circumstances help explain the Ceuta of yesteryear. Given the coast's inaccessibility, the mountain regions withdrew into themselves. Furthermore, between 1925 and 1956,[19] the region occupied by the Spaniards was long isolated by frontiers that separated it from the French Protectorate.

The history of Spain's colonial presence in Morocco has often been depicted as an unmitigated disaster, and has lacked any discussion of the improvements that took place during that period. To use a phrase of Karl Marx's, Spain at the time was the Asia of Europe, lacking in the resources of capitalist colonial powers. Therefore, in the Spanish zone, colonization limited itself to the all-out exploitation of the Rif's rich, dense forests. Spanish companies had a de facto monopoly on the exportation of timber to the Iberian Peninsula. Oak was used for the laying down of railways while cedar was used in construction. Eventually, mining became the dominant economic activity. Furthermore, the division of the country into the Spanish Protectorate in the north and the French Protectorate to the south encouraged the growth of smuggling between both zones.

At the time of independence, there were enormous expectations regarding amenities and jobs. The State, incapable of responding to the people's needs, followed a policy that turned out to be unproductive. Its management of the Riffian economy was centralized and based on procedures that were better suited to the country's southern regions. Are such criticisms without basis, given the country's needs at the national level? The State extended to the north the south's landholding regime, introduced restrictions on the right to use forest lands, imposed new taxes and severely repressed the culture of *kif*.[20] A diminution of revenues from abroad ensued, doubtless linked to fluctuations in contraband activity or to the diminution of emigration towards the west of

Algeria after the start of that country's armed struggle for independence.

The Riffian uprising of 1958–59 was a dramatic episode, the reverberations of which can be felt even today.[21] The Riffians paid a steep price for their rebellion, and the repression that ensued was fierce. To this day, the people of the Rif remain convinced that their region was deliberately excluded from public development projects by way of reprisal.

I've long been aware of what it means to be Riffian. When I used to attend Central Committee meetings of the political organization to which I belonged, the OADP, I had no idea that the roads that comrades who came to us from Al Hoceima were obliged to take were in such a terrible state. Unimaginably dangerous roads, essentially fragments of primitive roadway, really, all sorts of heights, ravines, bends, before finally coming upon Taza, then Fez, then Rabat . . . Moreover, transport vehicles were in a pitiful state and the trip was expensive. I speak from experience, having travelled along these routes several times since. In undertaking these journeys myself, I finally understood the trouble which being a Riffian member of a national political organization entailed.

Ultimately, the whole of the Rif can be regarded as a zone of barriers and borders created by the forces of nature as well as by public policies, or by the lack of public policies and by the inaction of the authorities. In contrast, the sea, which abuts the region's northern borders, seems like a much more readily surmountable obstacle. Much of the Rif is inhabited by settled mountain people in search of supplementary resources: historically, the craft industry was the backbone of the Riffian economy. Later, the mainstay became emigration, and perhaps *kif* too, or so they say.

During my stay of a few days in the Rif, I noticed that the region is being methodically opened up thanks to an entire ensemble of operations of truly enormous significance. Travelling along the main roadways, we can see a new map of the Rif being charted that consists of places whose names had been hitherto confined to the region's interior. Now the names are emerging from clandestinity to make up a hugely diverse itinerary: Izzennassne, Ben Chguer, Oued Kert, Amjou, Dar al Kabdani, Plage Ifry, Efoumossyn, Plage Boujbouja, Oued Sidi H'ssain, Port Sidi H'ssain, Sidi Amar Ou Moussa, Oued Sidi Salah, Oued Amakrane, Boudinar, Temssamane, Oued Tizighine, Oued Nou, Oued Rhiss, Oued Iberbouken . . .

At Ajdir, I give myself the pleasure of going for a splendid swim in this no-less-splendid corner of the country, which isn't so terribly different from the rest of the Rif except for the stickiness of its sand which is as fine as flour and which, like dust, covers everything it touches.

All the car parks in Morocco seem to have passed the word around: the fee for guarding cars is 5 dirhams, like in Rabat. In Rabat, however, the fee is negotiable, but not here, where, incidentally, the guards come from other towns: Khemisset, Kenitra . . . The tariff is strictly applied and every once in a while bitter quarrels break out over it . . .

I wonder: What's most important for people here? The elections? The new coastal road along the Mediterranean? The fact that it's summer? The function of elections as political safety valve, or the region's infrastructure? It's clear to me that the problems of representative democracy are far from most people's minds ...

On 5th August, I once again visit Al Hoceima's city centre. The Banque du Maroc branch in this town is probably one of the ugliest structures in the country. It resembles a police station implanted in a working-class quarter during the Years of Lead, a blockhouse on a permanent state of alert to ward off a threat that never materializes. Furthermore, the branch's surroundings are draped in red. State-decreed holidays succeed one another and an unbearable ambiance of Orientalist totalitarianism envelops the main square. With its surfeit of flags and unimaginative banners, Place Mohammed V resembles Moscow's Red Square during the heyday of socialism, in an environment where immigrants are only a fugitive and random presence.

Standards of service, the quality and value of the hotel supply and commercial relations all remain terribly unpredictable. If Morocco is going to become the tourist paradise it wants to become, it's going to have to improve its services ... Since leaving Rabat, I notice once again that what's vitally needed here is a cultural revolution of sorts. Again, the authorities ought to seriously concern themselves with raising standards across all fronts, from hygiene to manners to ethical norms ... Despite the abandonment to which they claim to have been subjected by the State, these tough mountain dwellers are essentially courteous and astute, and, while a culture steeped in stalemate can't be transformed overnight, people can be trained to adopt new ways ...

After the historic uprisings of the 1950s and their repression, the State tried a new approach to regional problems.

During a twenty-five-year span and in a territory of 2 million inhabitants divided into plots of integrated development, it implemented a variety of policies with priority given to the fight against erosion and the raising of incomes and revenues via agricultural modernization programmes. Instead of fostering real development, however, the project simply became a technical matter of erosion control.

The Sebou project was aimed at the modernization of another region, the Gharb, but it was tied to the Rif campaign and wagered on the prospect of the Rif's successful reforestation. The region's rural farm workers benefited from employment in the building sites that were launched with funds from international assistance programmes or from the State's budget for national development.

Yet another project aimed to provide an alternative impetus for the region's development. Centred on the idea that the forest still occupies a central place in the everyday lives of its inhabitants, and on the fear that the Rif's woodlands risk being overexploited and deforested, chiefly thanks to the tentacular spread of *kif* cultivation, the authorities set themselves the goal of protecting the region's green spaces. It was hoped that the attempt to recruit the Riffians to this scheme would help promote the anti-cannabis campaign.

Numerous threats to the Rif's forests have constantly loomed over the region. For instance, the Spanish Protectorate's priorities, and, since independence, the State's punitive neglect, have by turns fostered an excessive reliance on timber. Other threats include the ecological effects of the short-term farming that's always been practised around these parts (and that persistently requires the clearing of new terrain), the keeping of sizeable goat herds, demographic growth and the expansion of cannabis cultivation . . . The authorities have sometimes spoken to me about the efforts that they've undertaken to work with the local population in searching for supplementary solutions aimed at managing the Rif's resources more sustainably.

On the whole, the Rif would appear to be an environment conducive to agricultural development despite the manifest lack of arable land in a country that consists chiefly of steep slopes arranged in a variety of configurations. The effects of active erosion, of boreholes, of rock falls and landslides and the collapse of different structures are compounded by the creation of forest clearings which in turn are a consequence of an increasing population density thanks to the repeated influx of migrants and the expansion of cannabis cultivation. Moreover, the region would appear to lack much industry and to have a very limited fishery.

I meet with a young geography teacher at a secondary school in town. He explains how *kif* cultivation and its associated activities have grown phenomenally since the 1970s. High demand and a variety of ecological factors are behind the substantial rise in the price of cannabis. Well adapted to the Rif's soil, cannabis has a short growing season of around four months and can handle a variety of conditions: it can grow in irrigated soil and in non-irrigated soil and doesn't require any specific cultivation methods. What's more, its yield is high and its selling price is attractive to subsistence farmers.

I crisscross the region. In contrast to my previous visits, I notice considerable changes in infrastructure and basic amenities, in agriculture, in housing and labour conditions and in the forest sector . . . These days more people are at work in the Rif . . .

Emigration has historically been a major source of external revenue for the region. After the Souss, the Rif has for a long time been the country's largest exporter of people to foreign lands, chiefly Europe. The phenomenon began in the 1960s, and the establishment of immigrant networks in the host countries enabled increased emigration from the entire region to France, the Netherlands, Belgium, Germany and Spain.

The Rif's different sites are of a sublime beauty. (An article on the region by a geographer friend and colleague of mine puts it a bit more clinically: 'The coast is of a highly picturesque character.') Without a doubt, the littoral's role as tourist destination is becoming increasingly consistent, thanks to the increased demand for leisure activities and facilities on the part of visitors who are attracted to the Rif's beaches which, for the most part, are still intact and, for the time being at least, still affordable to low-income holidaymakers.

The 6th of August. I spend the day chatting with friends whom I regard as seasoned observers of the Rif. I've organized the day around several rendezvous and gatherings, during the course of which I have discussions with activists from civil society and the political parties, among them, of course, those who align themselves with the Amazigh movement. The questions we've broached have to do with the region's most pressing issues.

One of my interlocutors' central concerns is the Rif's status as an enclave. The Riffians are deeply affected by the fact that their region is isolated from the rest of the country. As a result, they've had to look after themselves, exercise a sort of de facto autonomy and orient themselves towards foreign countries.

My colleagues' remarks often turn on the past. In this part of the country, the Years of Lead began in the late 50s, shortly after independence, at the time of the notorious events of the Rif, of its population's successive paroxysms of protest, of the springing up of social movements throughout the region. A good number of stories attest to the continued relevance of that period. Moreover, the Amazigh Question has taken on new dimensions. Its expression by means of a newly burgeoning pro-autonomy culture is a real surprise for this observer. Clearly, we're witnessing a shift to an altogether different category of demands.

Internal immigration remains on the agenda. The Riffians living in poverty continue to seek better living conditions elsewhere in the country. New trends in the region's capitalist economy corroborate this tendency, for instance, with transfers being made to Rabat, Kenitra and Casablanca, according to the latest reports published by national banks that operate in the Rif. I note in passing the degree to which the aftermath of the 2004 earthquake evinces the centralizing culture of State power.

But what about the elections? At present, people's involvement in the elections and in the charting of a new political map seems weak. I've got everything I need in order to keep making inquiries about the elections (e.g. press kits, scholarly bibliography), and, wherever I go, I continue to conduct the sorts of interviews that are the stock-in-trade of social scientists. These interviews help me better understand the mechanisms of voting preferences. In all probability, we're not talking about a tendency that's specific to this part of the country. What we're talking about here is the role of regional bosses. It was explained to me that when a vote hunter arrives in a hamlet, he's referred to such and such a person who's been entrusted with the task of speaking on everybody's behalf. This role of intermediary, buying or selling votes or negotiating compromises for the next elections on behalf of a local collective, tends to be a specialized profession.

According to numerous accounts, in several parts of the region, votes cast for several candidates at once have been sold without leaving a money trail. Sometimes, money is given in exchange for guarantees . . . terms are discussed with the people and with the elites. Often, it's a question of deals being clinched between leading candidates.

On 7th August, I set out for Saâïdia from Al Hoceima in the midst of the bustle of summer. The faces I see in the Rif's capital are those I've seen throughout the country. On the return journey, I look up the different places I've visited in the order in which I've made a record of them. I note a stop at Arekmane to rest and to eat. And as is the case every time I visit, by eating there I run the risk of food poisoning. To walk around in Arekmane means to wage battle with its swarms of hellish flies as well as with an army of dodgy and sweaty waiters who take orders as they please and serve tables helter-skelter. They wait on you while dripping with sweat and so once again I find myself harping on the same refrain: we need to raise standards in this country . . . .

I drive in the direction of the country's eastern borders. For the first time I see from up close the three-storey islands (or to be more precise, rocks) which are still under Spanish rule.[22] From the coast, they look like the stuff of fables. However, they also strike me as yet another testimony to our age-old failures. We've handled the task of decolonization poorly in this country. We failed to liberate the totality of the national territory and these days we fail to follow through on the tasks that we set out to achieve. Even now, we're not succeeding at the task of developing the country more efficiently and quickly. We're not even making a token move in that direction . . .

My daughter's reaction upon seeing the islands couldn't be more nationalistic: 'But they're Moroccan!' On the radio, the stretch of road between Arekmane and Saâïdia sounds like a music box featuring tunes from all over the world, in all languages and rhythms. I let the needle on the radio tune in to whatever station it chooses . . .

Suddenly in the distance looms Fadesa, an immense housing estate that's currently under construction . . . It's an immense undertaking. Instinctively, I tell myself that plenty of people must be wondering whether there might not be a future scandal lurking behind all that. Oh how I wish I could free myself from this culture of deep mistrust that sees cabals, schemes and scandals everywhere! Nevertheless, the fact remains that this project is simply too big to be above-board. Everything we've lived through in recent years fosters this culture of wholesale distrust. In any case, aside from posing the sorts of questions which a citizenry that's become habituated to corruption at all levels tends to ask, I wonder about the project's financial viability. Is it positive or negative?

Although it seems like an oasis situated at the ends of the earth, from the moment you enter it, Saâïdia strikes the traveller as a town that's reached breaking point, deficient in infrastructure and upkeep, marred by all manner of short-comings and defects, its beaches bursting at the seams . . .

We desperately look for a place to stay. In vain, we check out several so-called hotels and guesthouses. It's the same story wherever we ask: no rooms available. Finally, we manage to find a passable inn which is graced with a decent coat of paint as well as a semblance of decor and a suggestion of orderliness. At 400 dirhams, it's cheap lodging for the night. We settle in, but the more time goes by the more the noise coming from the hotel's depths makes me realize the extent to which the place has gone to the dogs. By now I feel as though the whole town is unwholesome. I'm just going to spend the night here and then leave first thing in the morning.

Earlier, when I'd parked my car, the parking attendant had told me that he recognized me right away. 'Dr Saaf! I've often seen you on TV,' he said. Then congratulated me on my activism. I wasn't quite sure what he was talking about. My community work, in which I've immersed myself ever more deeply since the end of the first post–Hassan II government's term? Or was he specifically referring to my stint as a gov-ernment minister during the previous legislature's term of office? The fellow told me that he's from Khemisset and that he comes back to Saâïdia every summer to work as a seasonal car-park attendant. He describes how emigrants descend upon the town every summer. They spend their holidays here, and on the strength of their high earnings, afford themselves all the pleasures their money can buy, thereby disrupting this sleepy coastal resort's way of life. For a few weeks in the summer Saâïdia lives for, and off, their presence . . .

These Moroccans who live abroad have changed. They don't seem to care much about the elections. That, at any rate, seemed to be the last thing that the group of them whom I approached at the cafe were concerned about. Perhaps Morocco will eventually become for them one big holiday camp, or a simply a place that's connected with their personal pasts. As for the food, same story here as at Arekmane: dinner is totally unappetizing. Hygiene, the look of a place, its design: more work should go into improving all these things. This sort of thing can be learnt, can be inculcated. I suppose it's also a question of time. There's such a huge need for education, for training, for raising the level of the general culture . . .

I get a call from a journalist friend who's the head of one of our newspapers of record: 'Are you aware of what's just happened?' he asks. I learn that the deputy home secretary has just resigned and the king has accepted his resignation, thereby authorizing him to stand for election in the Ben Guérir electoral district.

This is stunning news! We Moroccans have become used to thinking about politics in terms of certain stock notions, such as that of the strongman who's so powerful that he never leaves office. We can't really conceive of a situation that isn't dominated by such a man. And the deputy home secretary was inevitably perceived as being just this sort of character, wielding influence as he did in security circles and in non-security circles alike, as well as in the worlds of politics and business. In telling me the news, my informant had quickly ventured the hypothesis that the fellow had in fact been dismissed. In his view, the story about the deputy home secretary's standing for election was just a face-saving ploy in the face of the media's relentlessly repeated refrain that the central government—which has had to deal with plenty of such types—had decided to rid itself of this neo-vizier.

This event brought to mind a similar occasion, the dismissal of Driss Basri on 8th November 1999, his birthday.[23] Except this time around we're not talking about a decision by the authorities to dismiss a functionary from his post. Instead, this appears to be a case of voluntary and considered departure. In any case, the event is certainly consequential, coming as it does on the eve of the elections and the second round of negotiations over the Western Sahara's future. The official in question had taken part in the first round of talks and his name had been mentioned in news about the delegation that would shortly launch the next round of discussions at Manhasset.[24] After all, that wouldn't be a contradictory state of affairs . . . I'm wary, yet optimistic. I think that the coming days are going to yield new perspectives on this matter.

Wherever we go, we notice a large number of Moroccan emigrants visiting from other countries. The watchman, with whom I have long discussions about the elections here and at Khemisset, tells me that in ten days' time there'll be nobody around till next summer.

The emigrants sitting at nearby tables seem impervious to the questions I ask them about the elections. Because the light in our room is so faint, I try reading Ismail Kadaré's *The Pyramid*[25] in a corner of the cafe's terrace that's set back from the main area. Near my table, emigrants to Belgium and the Netherlands quarrel angrily and exchange insults and threats that have nothing to do with the ballot. Instead, their shouting match turns on sex, booze and cars, on getting engaged and then breaking up, on getting married and divorcing, on bad blood and on food, on prices, purchases and deals . . .

I go to sleep, and am awoken when the night-club closes in the early hours and its clients spill out into the hotel's rooms. I stay up reading till morning, pack my bags early, check out at the earliest occasion and leave behind the drab resort . . .

On this 8th August, I head out of Saâïdia by taking the road to Oujda that passes through Ahfir. Upon sighting Algerian flags on the other side of the road, the territories of Algeria and Morocco strike me as being tangled up in one another, but things must be thus in all borderlands. On this occasion, my heart clenches in a different way than it did when I saw the little bits of Moroccan soil still occupied by Spain. We Moroccans of the Atlantic coast are accustomed to regarding the sea as the country's natural boundary or, rather, as a non-boundary. I'm used to thinking of the country in terms of limitless expanses, vast areas and no frontiers. Is this what opponents of the Western Sahara territory's integration into the country's administrative structure call Moroccan 'annexationism' or 'expansionism'? Well, I've decided that after leaving Ahfir, to which I'm returning for the umpteenth time, I won't drive up to Berkane but, instead, will head to the interior. This inclination towards isolationism, towards adopting an inward-looking attitude, is an old habit of mine, a familiar reflex towards intrusive things, a habitual reaction to the Other who comes too close. As it happens, this tendency is also a trait of my country's political culture which shrinks into itself and into insularity at the same time as it, paradoxically, encounters the open sea.

6.
RABAT–CASABLANCA

9th August, Rabat–Casablanca

I've just met with a journalist I know who recently interviewed the civil servant who's stepped down and who tells me that the fellow has confirmed the official version of events. But, he added, the functionary's deeply disappointed air seemed to belie his affirmations. In fact, his statements seem incompatible with a good number of declarations he's made lately. My 'informant' remarked that he thought he noticed hints of despondency in the man's affect. Over the course of the interview, the latter conveyed the impression that he'd been treated unjustly. Moreover, he seemed to be complaining that the powers that be were being ungrateful towards him given all that he'd achieved over the past few years.

As for me, the press keeps asking me for my reading of the event. I refuse to comment on situations about which I'm ill informed. I don't think I've got enough facts at my disposal to answer their questions, so I've been hedging. However, my refusal to provide the press with comments doesn't mean that I don't have my own thoughts about the case. Here are some of them:

What we may be dealing with here might not in fact be a punitive action levelled against an official but, rather, a tactic deployed to save one of the regime's men, who, perhaps despite himself, and doubtless against his will and that of the regime, has reproduced a model of governance that has so often been denounced. This is a man who became too powerful, who without really wanting to forgot himself went so far as to act like a lord and master. The wielding of too much power ineluctably leads the wielder to abuse it ... His departure was probably rendered unavoidable by an accumulation of negative comments regarding his administration's authoritarian tics.

The outgoing official is a playing card in the great game of politics whom the head of state has momentarily set aside in order to later make use of him as needed. In this light, he's a decisive resource who for the time being is being kept in reserve.

Since he knew the people who are now at the centre of this situation, it's not out of the question that they might want to give the impression that they're above any sort of authoritarianism. Their current authoritarianism could then be read as no more than a passing and historically necessary phase, and the official's resignation would be proof that they're not obsessed by the prospect of power. On that note, I remember that when I visited Iraq in 1991 after Bush Sr's war, a member of a group of intellectuals received by Saddam Hussein asked him if he intended to carry out 'democratic' reforms. The Master of Baghdad responded by saying that he wasn't power-hungry but merely a champion of a great cause, the standard bearer of the Great Arab Renaissance ...

The papers are still soliciting my opinions regarding the recent event, but I keep avoiding them since I don't think that the affair can yet be the subject of credible commentary. These sorts of incidents nearly always entail dimensions that are too obscure for any analysis or the staking out of a pertinent position. For the time being, I lack access to far too many bits of important information ...

10th August.

I continue undertaking my survey of the state of the nation on the eve of national elections by means of face-to-face meetings with a variety of people in cafes, hotels, offices, homes ... Naturally, my interviews focus on the mood of the country during this electoral period.

I meet with candidates for office. Their state of mind is an important indicator of how things are going. On the whole, what I'm hearing is that things are still gestating and that the majority of them are still operating at the level of preparatory and organizational meetings. Are a few hours' worth of chitchats with the citizenry enough to convince them to vote for you? Can a few leaflets printed in haste by overbooked printers who are attending to requests from all sides suffice to get your message out?

There's no doubt about it, the mobilization of the voters is proceeding at a slow rhythm and is barely visible.

11th August.

I suddenly find myself in the rural areas of the capital's hinterland. The weather at Rommani is extremely hot, the sun is blazing in the sky, and once again there's a police checkpoint on the way out of town.

In light of certain exchanges between lorry drivers on the one hand and law-enforcement officials on the other, I can't help thinking, wrongly no doubt, that this mobilization of the police force comes as a windfall which allows them to engage in acts of petty corruption. Not even the fear of terrorism seems to prevent them from doing so. Is everybody in this country corrupt, corrupting or corruptible?

For the first time on this route, I come across a service area attached to a petrol station. In this place, which by definition is polluted, people freshen up. Green spaces, leisure activities and good morning coffee.

The field I'm working in here isn't that of history, or sociology, or administrative zoning. The places I'm visiting are recreated and revisited by the researcher. First, the municipality of Hmaza. Its mosque's imam is very welcoming and kindly invites us to tea. He can tell that I'm seeking something, that I'm looking for information, yet he doesn't ask any questions. In contrast to what usually happens in similar circumstances, he doesn't seem to harbour any suspicions towards me. His words give evidence of a certain political awareness. His appearance and bearing convey an impressive self-assurance of the kind that I'm incapable of feeling in these sorts of situations. Here, everything takes place far from the gaze of the State. Without thinking about it too much, along the route I start taking photos of the mosques that line the roadway. And then I cross the stream.

This region interests me utterly and the area's Tamazight toponymy fascinates me. Tamazight is a fascinating creation.

The research team to which I belong worked on a project for this zone, the Zaër, for an institute that promotes Amazigh culture and language. The project's aim was to create a more precise linguistic and cultural map of the region. However, the institute rejected the proposal. We were reminded that, according to its founding documents, the institute was created for the advancement of the Tamazight language. Their letter claimed, a touch peremptorily, that, except for its western zones, the Arab area of the Zaër didn't form part of the Amazigh sphere. We undertook our research nevertheless, and the results of our inquiry categorically contradicted the letter's presuppositions. We discovered that the presence of Tamazight language and culture was equally strong through the territory and that they were interwoven with Moroccan Arabic.

The cars that drive along these roads are often old models, vestiges of decades gone by, automobiles belonging to returning emigrants . . . Combined with the remaining houses from the colonial era, these vintage vehicles lend the prevailing atmosphere a curious air. A straightforward sort of utilitarianism pervades these spaces. The signposts refer to precise distances: Oued Zem is 100 km away. Moreover, the region's ambience and the people with whom I speak strike me as being strongly rooted in local affairs. I spend most of my time meeting with such people.

In driving around the Zaër region I notice its specific agricultural features: doum palms in the midst of cultivated cereal crops, evermore numerous olive groves. And here is a new mosque—or rather, prayer hall—with a minaret overlooking the road. It's small, clean and quiet and is built right up against a modest home. Moreover, the place of worship and dwelling place combine with a water tower to create an ensemble of integrated elements. Farther along, a prison rears up in the middle of the rural landscape like a fortress looming over the wheat fields. Families that clearly come from several different parts of the country wait for the visiting hours to start.

On the road, countless labourers are busily engaging in renovations which have no doubt been prompted by the election season. A whole host of projects get launched on such occasions, e.g. the construction of public fountains, water mains, roadwork . . . all of which would seem to be linked to the elections . . .

I juggle a variety of contradictory impressions. Given the diversity of its circumstances, the multiple strategic analyses of the region shouldn't advance one single overview of its character and needs but take several viewpoints into consideration. It's not just that the topics to be addressed vary from one *douar* to another. It's also that the content of ostensibly identical topics differs too. The diversity of strategic analyses of the needs of the region's inhabitants, of their priorities, of their hopes and suffering, makes me think that a proper vision of our society's development should take on the state of the nation as a whole while making room for the specific conditions prevailing in every one of its constituent parts.

Moreover, it seems impossible to distinguish one project from another. Everybody seems to be saying the same thing and making the same sort of proposal but without making clear how what they're proposing is relevant, and, above all, convincing.

Along the way I encounter a mobile banking shop. Is it a simple coincidence that it's popped up at election time? A researcher has drawn up a study of microcredit in the region and it appears that this method of accessing funds has really taken off. In these parts, souk (market) days don't see much activity during the summer months. Peasants also take summer holidays.

I'm told by some that, during this electoral period, little money seems to be circulating in the rural areas, at least around here. Others tell me that we're witnessing a novelty, the decline of the money economy. At the same time, informed observers point out that new ways of using money are being put into effect. It would appear that the relationship between elections and politics is no longer reducible to the circulation of large sums of cash. The system of electoral observers currently in place isn't strong enough to preclude fraud. Nevertheless, the candidates take precautions. Although in certain towns it's possible to have totally fair and clean elections, the same can't be said about the countryside.

Another attitude I notice in my chats with those who are keen to talk about the elections is that people tend to think of the candidates as though they'll exercise a form of executive power. They ask themselves, 'What's this fellow going to be able to give us?'

Then there's the fact that there are few or no debates. Silence reigns. We're not even talking about a situation in which the politicians brush aside accountability reports. Here, such reports are neither presented to the electorate nor brushed aside.

According to the classic model of democratic governance, forms of government should be judged by the governed, and this judgement ought to weigh heavily in the decision-making process. I recall some lines by John Berger—among many other statements about the nature of democracy—in which he speaks of ordinary democratic societies and their particular ills. In his view, a dialectic of discussion replaced unconditional, and therefore undemocratic, submission on the part of the governed. If, however, the candidates don't expound on their point of view nor clearly explain what actions they would undertake if elected, if all of this remains unsaid and unread, then the electorate, Berger concludes, can't fulfil its dialectic democratic role, since there is no real dialogue over essential questions. When a candidate lacks a roadmap, or claims not to have one, the voters are reduced to serving as mere workhorses. A conspiracy of silence results in tacit agreements. Citizens are transformed into clients, and debates are reduced to competitions between styles. In a situation in which so-called opinion polls are valued more highly than proposals for transforming society, self-promotion becomes the order of the day. In any case, the elections seem so remote from people's concerns that wherever I've travelled there's been little evidence of competition among candidates and no opinion polls have been carried out . . .

In ordinary democratic situations, the different candidates would address the various fears that different sectors of the population feel. They would also attend to the impact that particular policies have had on the voters, all the while promising not to forget them. They could do all this while not referring for a moment to the totality of the situation and without asking what's happening in the wider world. In our elections, however, I don't sense any fears, any anguish or any evidence of what far-too-distant observers refer to as 'exchanges over potential stakes'.

In universal terms, history entails discussions over the nature of events, their causes and consequences, as well as debates over margins of manoeuvre, all of which are then followed by the outlining of a political vision. In the absence of such deliberations, promises made to the voters are likely to fall short. In the final analysis, the outcome of such an election would be to obliterate the complex experiences of history, to efface the past and to constrain political choices to whatever happens to be on sale at the moment.

During this time, the sole effective actor—the State and its organs—will debate its development project (dubbed 'modern-democratic') with itself. I've already noted that the head of state has been active throughout the pre-election period, as if reminding the country of the primacy of his bond with the people, and that his position is situated somewhere beyond the democratic order. In any case, the prevailing view is that much will be done outside the elected administration's sphere of activity. Ten million tourists, a thouand engineers a year, large infrastructure works, ten thousand development workers, the creation of thousands of jobs in the medium term—these are some of the upper limits that have been set for goals that have never before been of such magnitude and which we keep being urgently reminded of . . . Nevertheless, the fact remains that these ambitious aims could be stalled by systemic limitations: the prevailing authoritarianism, lack of resources, cultural backwardness, the glaring gap between us and our Spanish neighbours to the north, a project which bills itself 'modern-democratic' but which doesn't include too many authentic democrats or consistent modernizers . . .

On that very day, I get back home to Rabat in the late afternoon. I've got a rendezvous with Khatibi.[26] My discussions with him are always edifying. We're particularly interested in the matter of voter participation. The question of the electorate's participation in the upcoming elections has motivated all actors, be they associated with the State or with the political parties, 'democrats of all persuasions'.

There's been a conspicuous diminution in the turnout. With the proviso that the administration may have massaged the data, we can note that whereas in the previous election there'd been a turnout of 52 per cent, in the five years since then the participation has fallen to 37 per cent. Moreover, the same abstention figures have been noted since 1962, namely, a million spoilt ballots at each election, except for the most recent one in 2002 when the number was around 700,000. In any case, it's clear there's been a progressive dwindling of the turnout.

Increasing numbers of people have been adopting a non-participatory stance without regard to the degree of politicization that's been achieved up to this point, and without thinking much about what opting out of politics means for the public interest. Many have decided to tune out. Others have opted for exiling themselves in the politics of other nations. An example of this is the manner in which some people follow French, Spanish or European politics as though they were citizens of those polities. This pathological monitoring of the political life of other societies strikes me as an all-too-easy substitute for engagement with our own. Some have fled the field of national politics and plunged into the event-driven de-territorialized flux created by the mass media around such sites as Palestine, Iraq, Afghanistan or other identity-politics hotspots that attract the mass media's attention.

Since few stakeholders cultivate an authentic political project, non-participation is quite likely to worsen. Without any anchorage in such a project, we will surrender ourselves to the global centres where political and other forms of representation are generated, to the point where all we'll see in the suicide bombers that may emerge from this situation are minor forms of turbulence in the international political order. Simultaneously isolated and globalized, at sea in a soulless political world, adrift in the frantic politics of our time, a politics lacking in any genuine dialectical thrust, we're given lessons in morality by the powerful and any Johnny-come-lately and we let ourselves slide ineluctably towards an apolitical future.

I have a conversation with an independent journalist. My highly sceptical interlocutor addresses me with the air of somebody who long ago had everything sorted out. 'What is it you're going to be observing?' he asks. 'The voting system, the review of the electoral rolls, the drawing up of electoral boundaries, the entire organization of the ballot—all of these things were wrapped up long before you set out on your mission. What you're going to be observing doesn't account for more than 20 per cent of the whole operation, so what's the point?'

At any rate, electoral fraud probably won't be a matter of the ballot box. Almost everywhere, the selection of candidates has been undertaken in a legally hazy manner . . . I'm struck by the oft-repeated assertion by Islamists that good Muslims don't step forward as candidates for office. 'It's inconceivable that one of our militants should say, "I want to run for this or that position,"' I'm told. The expression of such a desire would be construed as proof of the illegitimacy of their aspirations. Elections aside, the same unwillingness applies to applications for administrative positions. It's an activist's friends and colleagues who urge and even beg him to occupy the post.

This state of mind harkens back to the attitudes of those of us who were active on the left in the good old days. For our part, we had no need of Quranic verses or sayings of the Prophet in order to declare our faith. Things have really changed since then. Will our Islamist comrades of all stripes escape the fate that befell us? I rather doubt it . . .

7.
FROM LARACHE TO
FNIDEQ VIA TANGIERS

On this 12th August, I begin my journey to the country north of Larache with a stopover at Asilah. What must the numerous European tourists walking in our midst think of our upcoming elections? And what must our own burgeoning middle classes think of them, our middle classes who haven't quite adjusted to their middling status and are therefore not quite 'middle class' or are still in the process of finding their feet in a middle-class world?

The infrastructural inconsistencies, the sparseness of leisure activities and the shortcomings in management and in logistics that were so abundantly evident at Saâïdia or Arekmane are also noticeable here, even though things are slightly improved in these parts and the town is better organized. Nevertheless, the place badly needs a general overhaul, albeit gently undertaken and without a concomitant loss of soul.

Here too there are no clearly discernible traces of the upcoming ballot. The presence of the elections is neither strongly felt nor totally absent. There's a sort of 'superimposition' of politics on all categories of thinking and doing (work, the economy, religion), like the imposition of morality on all the various dimensions of human life (political, religious, economic, cultural . . .) according to certain realist philosophers.

Tangiers, 13th August. While taking my morning coffee, I read the press. I spend some time catching up on the notes I've made over the past few days, and, after writing for a while, I leave my place late to go for a walk around the city before I get back to work.

The press publicizes the status of the negotiations at Manhasset. They seem belaboured. Something strange is cooking.

Since the weekend, the only topic on people's lips is the scandal involving the mayor of Rabat. Last Thursday evening, the police descended on his home. Eighty guests were forcibly taken to the police station while others fled the scene. The reasons for the raid were clearly stated: he began his electoral campaign prematurely, a crime made worse by his use of municipal resources (cars, the deployment of officials and staff to organize celebrations for nobody knows what purpose exactly . . .). The newspapers report that guests have been questioned and fined and that legal proceedings have been initiated . . . The incident has cast a spotlight on undertakings that are not always visible but that are widely practised nonetheless. This time around, we also have the emergence of an electoral police.

In theory, the pre-campaign is decisive. The most remarkable thing about the elections is that everybody who's engaged in campaigning has been doing so in advance. Preparations for the campaign have been underway well before the official starting date. In the rural areas, essential matters have already been settled. With their souks, their moussems,[27] their marriages and their extensive family connections, candidates from the countryside seem best suited to take advantage of pre-campaign electioneering. The means of communication used in the city (billposting, meetings, etc. . . .) aren't suitable out in the country. During the pre-campaign season, rural candidates are more at ease than their urban counterparts. Once the campaign proper kicks in, it buttresses their hold over their constituencies.

The papers also quote a curious injunction by the secretary general of the Istiqlal Party:[28] 'We want to conduct a clean electoral campaign. Be vigilant when you talk on your mobile phones. Limit the length of the calls and since we're being targeted, insist on the probity of your campaign.' Journalists often interpret this comment as a warning signal: 'If you cheat, do so carefully. You're under surveillance, so don't allow yourselves to get caught.'

The recent elections for the replacement of the outgoing third of the House of Councillors[29] seems to have had notable consequences, such as the launching of a 'clean hands' campaign and the annulment of elections. The results have been mixed. Several parties, among which the Istiqlal, the USFP and the PPS . . . have seen certain of their candidates sentenced on charges of corruption.

As happens at the start of every day, first thing in the morning I write while I have my cup of coffee, update my notes on the elections, go for my regular morning walk and then head back to my lodgings.

A bit later, I exit Tangiers via Cap Malabata, a narrow piece of land that overhangs the far north-western end of the

African continent, and a landmark to the north of which there's no more land but an easy-to-drive-along roadway which heads eastward. The bird seller who hasn't shifted from his spot in years is still there. For more than ten summers, I've seen him standing in the same place, and I'm tempted to buy a couple of birds from him as I did years ago when I bought a couple of canaries. For several years, the two kept us company, close to my study. One day, one of them died, and as if ineluctably, the other one followed suit a few days later . . .

The drive is nice and easy and gives onto splendid views. Spain, the Spanish coast, the maritime route to that other world are clearly visible this morning. What is it about the other shore that makes it more appealing? Without hurrying too much, in little more than half an hour we arrive in Ksar El Kbir. I spend a little while by the sea before I restart my enquiry. We get settled in on the beach, which is situated just a short walk away from the centre of this small town. I've been coming here since Ksar El Kbir was a little village. The water's nice and lovely and cool. This beach makes the sea seem like a swimming pool. Every so often, the water's surface is gently ruffled by a pleasant breeze. The sun is hot, but it's not stifling as it was in Al Hoceima.

Life in the greater Tangiers zone is bound up with life in many other places. The city itself, whose hinterland is delimited by Fahs province, conveys the impression of being peninsular, outward-looking, overcrowded. It has the appearance of a promontory jutting outwards towards Spain, Gibraltar, Europe . . . This year its population has risen to over 700,000 inhabitants, and human migration from the Rif continues unabated . . . Tangiers is also a central node in the clandestine migratory routes to Europe.

Urbanization in the greater Tangiers zone is uneven and whether or not it conforms to regulations depends on the specific area we're talking about. Neighbourhoods built without the State's approval keep expanding. Everywhere, a survival economy is the order of the day, alongside much entrepreneurial activity. All of this seems to lend greater value to the city's historic quarter and to its periphery, in contrast to its industrial zones.

Bordering both the Atlantic and the Mediterranean, Tangiers clearly aspires to become a metropolis. However, it's also clear that it hasn't completely shed its role as a city of transit. While it hasn't yet attained metropolitan status, it seems to be in the process of becoming an important industrial centre with strong banking facilities. New investments have been made in the region thanks to the fiscal advantages that the State has granted it over the past decade. Like the industrial zone, the free-trade zone stands out like a city within a city. As for the tourist areas around the bay, here as elsewhere they do their own thing. The hotel industry's entire infrastructure seems equivalent in size to that of Casablanca. Moreover, the textile and clothing industry has also taken root here, even though it's still a bit precarious, dependent as it is on foreign markets and on decision-makers in Casa . . . In contrast to the passenger port, the cargo port seems fairly modest in size. International organizations have also established a presence in Tangiers, although they're not terribly active. Finally, Tangiers is home to the Medi-I radio station, whose listeners tune in avidly from around the entire Maghreb.

Summertime in Tangiers is always a stifling melange of the chergui[30] typical of the whole region and of hot weather, politics, smuggling, crime, misdemeanours, cement, polluted beaches and bathers drowned and saved. In this little gulf, the sands are hot, the winds are strong and the entire landscape is cluttered with plastic bags of different colours. I wonder whether the fact that the bags are now predominantly black signifies a positive change from the preceding decade. Then, the predominant colour was white.

A major event at Meknes: a man has blown himself up close to a tourist coach. I concentrate instead on the interview with El Yazghi[31] published in *Ach-Charq Al Awsat*.[32] He explains the reasons for the withdrawal of his candidacy from the elections. 'Yes, we're fielding new party members,' he states. (For 'candidates' he uses the word *moultahiqqin*, by which he means candidates who've switched over from other parties.) But not everybody who's previously held administrative positions is bad or corrupt. I recall an observation by Robert Kagan[33] to the effect that not all dictatorships are inherently iniquitous.

With regard to the voting system, the socialist leader believes that it makes room for all political tendencies and prevents any one from obtaining an absolute majority. 'The current coalition government's track record is strong not only in general terms but also in terms of the specific reforms it's carried out. We don't have a problem with the possibility that the current coalition might continue to govern.' The parties of the ruling majority have overlapping programmes.

El Yazghi insists on various points. He notes that in addition to the fact that the USFP's programme resembles that of many other parties, the current majority coalition is the only one whose programmes resemble one another and the only one which can continue to make up a parliamentary majority and be in session. This idea is interesting enough, but it can hardly be deemed credible. For one thing, its proponent is deeply involved in the circumstances he describes. Furthermore, although on the face of it the assertion may seem irrefutable, epistemologically speaking it's unverifiable and indemonstrable and therefore even more suspect . . . If all the parties resemble one another and advance the same programme, what would prevent other parties from forming a majority? The proposition is so very general that it boomerangs on its advocate. If all of the electable parties and their respective programmes are alike, then surely the situation is ripe for the arrival on the scene of a force or a grouping with different characteristics and, what is more, quite capable of taking the helm.

This reasoning prompts me to rethink the question of what the best vision for our society should look like. It's possible that the close resemblance between the various party programmes could attest to the existence of a common vision for the country, one that would be the object of unanimous agreement among the parties. Alternatively, it could be read as evidence of a large consensus in favour of a common programme, or simply the product of an agreement reached by a relative majority, one that would only exclude a few groups of individuals—or even some organizations—who keep a critical distance between themselves and the political system.

In my view, however, the strong resemblance between the programmes demonstrates the lack of a global vision among the parties in question, unless by 'global vision' one means an array of certitudes culled from the World Bank's credo.

From the latter standpoint, the remaking of Morocco, and indeed its salvation, would best be left in the hands of the king. *This* vision of our national destiny corresponds to the official view outlined in the pages of the Fiftieth Anniversary Report, and in its explicit or implicit messages, a report which has been transformed into one of the new monarch's major political projects . . .

What all of this means is that a vision or visions of society are still in need of articulation . . . and as a result of this state of affairs, the notion of a vision of society is to some degree mystified and remains in the background as a kind of idyllic reference point.

It remains to be asked what margin of manoeuvre the international order permits us. Nobody seems to be in command of the relevant facts. It's a matter of focus. A pragmatic vision of society has to analyse the consequences of globalization for all aspects of our national life . . . All around me, in this Moroccan August of 2007, there's no sign that my fellow Moroccans are debating these matters in the public sphere. Instead, what we've got is small-scale electoral activity among individuals.

I've noted reflections on other subjects: Islamists, the democratic method, the question of the Sahara, etc. I tell myself that I set out on this trip precisely to get away from the habitual prattle surrounding these topics . . .

In the press and in remarks I hear all around me, campaigns launched before the official starting date are being increasingly denounced as premature operations that avail themselves of public resources in order to influence voters, that supply illicit electoral promises and that don't abide by the rules of the electoral game (see the 16th August editions of *Al Massaa* and *L'Economiste*[34]). But how can we be certain that a certain activity actually constitutes an instance of fraudulent pre-campaigning? What's the definition of 'premature electoral campaign'? Among other things, the phrase refers to the use of public places, or, to be more precise, those spaces reserved for the posting of bills before the official start of the electoral season. Where do illicit electoral promises begin and where do electoral programmes which have become public end?

Should a party leader who ceaselessly discusses his political programme before, during and after the elections be sued? Gifts, largesse, promises of largesse, administrative favours, whether to a local collective or to a group of citizens, are gaining ground. Nevertheless, the general picture is varied. There have been a variety of collateral incidents in the news, such as the sentencing of a journalist who has written articles on security issues. Likewise, there's much discussion of an inquiry into the activities of former inmates of the Salafiya Jihadiya[35] group who have been released from prison at the same time as the country is on security alert.

As was the case yesterday, today I drive along the coast and pass by Ksar Esseghir. Tanger-Med port seems to be close to completion.[36] Terrible machines grind down the hills and level the surrounding plains, punch holes in the mountains and move the valleys, rendering the landscape uniform and free of any eccentric features. The essential outlines of the future monster are clearly visible. Nature continues to resist but is almost a spent force. Soon, she'll be in no position to prevail over the large contingent of workers that labour on this site . . .

I've driven along this route for years. I've travelled along the foothills of its majestic heights and its thrusting cliffs. I've frequented its timeless coves where in bygone days only a few traditional women bathed with all their clothes on so that no part of their bodies would show. The region's rolling hills, its solemn mountains, its unevenly wooded zones, its almost wild natural environment are all now being crushed, flattened, furrowed, turned upside down, moulded and remade by monstrous engines that resemble an invading army. Here, the way in which human beings break down the natural world takes on strange overtones. One gets the impression that it won't be coming to an end anytime soon.

A bit farther looms the border town of Fnideq, whose identity includes, but isn't reducible to, a thriving contraband trade and black market. Its centre envelops and swallows up the traveller. It seems to be jampacked with outsiders. Holidaymakers go the beach in the daytime, and then, by mid-afternoon, shop till they drop. I should have bypassed the town, although perhaps it's important to get the measure of the elections in a place like this. Under the hot sun, endless traffic jams cause cars to grind to a halt for long moments . . .

The region appears to be in the midst of an explosive demographic growth. Its various parts serve as an emporium through which circulate contraband products from Spain, as well as Moroccan fish products. All in all, the place strikes me as a huge and disorganized entrepôt, located in the heart of a vast quasi-informal network of distribution and refurbishment.

8

FROM FNIDEQ TO TETOUAN

Soon we arrive at Almina beach, on the outskirts of Fnideq. I have a coffee in a quiet beachside spot under the blazing sun. The sea is beautiful and intensely blue, a pure, limpid blue of a transparency that one can't find elsewhere. By chance, I run into the director of a centre for European strategic studies located in Paris and regarded as one of the most influential think tanks in the world. He arrived some days ago to participate in the annual summer symposium of the Asilah Forum Foundation and has since been joined by his family for a brief holiday.

We discuss the burning issues of the day—national and international—with the expert and his wife, especially the inescapable question of Morocco's democratization. They've read miscellaneous news items in the press, in particular stories about the convictions handed down to people who took part in disturbances on 1st May. In my view, they've formed opinions about the process underway across the nation a touch too readily. They tell me that they can't help but wonder if all the claims about bolstering human rights and democracy amount to little more than humbug. I find their views exaggerated.

I don't deny the possibility that a foreign observer might be able to grasp the truth of a given political situation, whether it be Morocco's or any other country's ... But I've become sceptical of assessments that are either too positive or too negative. Often, these viewpoints are the outcome of brief seasonal visits and of quick exchanges with select contacts who are likely to lead the observers away from the truth of things.

My interlocutor also noted the press's problems with the State and the State's problems with the press, a mere month away from Morocco's legislative elections. For instance, the editor of two weeklies has been charged with 'breach of the respect owed to the head of state' and will appear in court for his last editorial in which he reproached the monarch for unduly (in the journalist's view) concentrating too much power in his own hands and portraying himself as the guarantor of democracy.

This incident comes at a time of strained relations between part of the national press and the authorities. Two journalists who write for an Arabic-language weekly, *Al Watan*, are being taken to court for having 'misappropriated confidential documents concerning State security'. Such episodes are connected with the ongoing security alert, evidence of which they've seen on their travels, and which strikes them as an important subject in need of interpretation. My friends interpret these incidents as facts that evince the country's problematic transition to democracy.

In their view, the large-scale public-works projects widely in evidence around the region seem to infuse the authorities with greater confidence and push them towards more authoritarianism ... Might these projects therefore not reveal a certain regressive tendency, they wonder? If this is indeed so, then why in the case of Greece, Spain, Portugal, etc. did similar enterprises seem to consolidate those countries' democratic development, I ask myself, and why would that not be the case here?

Everybody talks about the Years of Lead, the strategist noted ... In response, I ponder the following questions: Do those who didn't live through that period have the right to talk about it without taking due precautions? Does historical conscience allow them to refer to it, and do they have the moral right to do so? Is the path that leads from collective memory to individual memory as direct as all that? Can a single individual's memory claim collective memory as his or her own, even though no individual can be aware of all of its constituent memories? The much-maligned authoritarian regime, accused of all wrongs, was itself the product of a certain social process. Is it right to speak about our past without having been an essential part of it, or without it having been an important and directly connected part of ourselves?

The whole debate over authoritarianism and democratization remains problematic. In none of the countries that I'm aware of is there a sufficiently reliable measure of the degree to which a regime is authoritarian enough to clearly determine how much 'lead' went into the making of our famous 'Years of Lead'. Academic protocols can confer a relative legitimacy to the discussion. But is it enough to know about a phenomenon to speak about it in a legitimate sort of way, or does one need to have lived through it?

I meet a young political commentator from Tetouan to discuss the elections in his city. He gives me the lowdown: there's been a dramatic turn of events regarding the Socialist Party's candidates. The party's general secretary has just parachuted in his assistant to replace the socialists' so-called Barons of the North. In acting thus, the party's executive has sought to counter the network of notables who have got hold of the region . . . The situation is virtually identical with that of the Istiqlal party: my colleague cites the case of a worthy who belongs to this organization. Whatever their partisan affiliation may be, all 'trans-partisan' corporations act alike . . .

The prominent candidates collude to a considerable extent. Let's assume that there are two important candidates, each of whom seems to have at their disposal a hard core of voters who support their respective candidacies. Speculation has it that in wards where the outcome is certain, the two will reach an agreement that will enable them to preserve their stalwarts. This pact will oblige them to support each other in certain districts in various ways: by dividing up adverse votes, by distributing votes among major and minor candidates, by buying and selling votes, by bribing authorities and candidates . . .

The RNI's situation is mixed. One of its leading candidates was also caught *in flagrante* during the pre-electoral campaign, but his malfeasance carried no adverse repercussions for him . . . The PJD seems to be the only solid force in the region, one which hasn't had to suffer the consequences of candidates being parachuted in . . . The outgoing deputy, who's well established in the area, has every chance of being re-elected . . . Corruption's stain taints departing candidates of both the Left and of the Right. Everybody has been commenting on how corrupt these officials were and on how their corruption de-legitimized their incumbency ...

In Tetouan, the role played by the city's notables seems inescapable. But are things really any different in numerous other corners of the country? Local politics is in the hands of Tetouan's venerable families, of the *zawiyas*,[37] of people who wield authority of one sort or another, and of those who enjoy the State's backing. At election time, the State avails itself of this network, as do the political parties and candidates of the Left. That's what they say about the young left-wing candidate. He's personally uncorrupted and above suspicion but he's certain to have obtained the support of those circles, support which would be strictly unacceptable to the left-wing rank and file. The *zawiyas*, whose role in the local elections is decisive, have invested a great deal of money both in the region and beyond, with extensive ramifications. Often, the State consults them.

On the whole, I get the same impression here as I've got elsewhere: although the elections are only a few weeks away, they're being regarded with a strange indifference and curious detachment. The voters aren't involved in preparing for them to any significant degree and the atmosphere is wan and lethargic. Even though the national interest may be at stake, who can get excited about choosing candidates in August, at the height of the beach season, when there are so many other choices to be made, such as which beach to go to, which imported bathing costumes to wear (while veiled women wade into the water with all their clothes on), which fizzy drink and sparkling water to imbibe? What's more, according

72

to the authorities themselves, not too many voters have obtained their voter-registration cards . . .

Instead of referring to the replacement of elites, we should speak of the replacement of candidates from the establishment's upper echelons: to assure themselves of a clean conscience, the authorities want to recuse candidates with an unsavoury record, according to the criteria upheld by the new men of honour. However, a communiqué from the Ministry of the Interior would seem to belie this aim. My interlocutor tells me that while the authorities would want to recuse such candidates, they can't do so readily. A.M., with whom I usually meet up when I'm in the area, considered running as an independent, but the authorities brought out three files showing he had signed false documents thrice . . .

Legions of holidaymakers have already headed home. Now we're in the period when some people prolong their holidays. Moroccans from 'the interior', which is what northerners call southerners, have come and gone between the end of July and mid-August.

In terms of the economy, 2007 seems to have been a good year for the region. The days when people up north lived off crumbs left behind by holidaymakers of limited means are long gone. I'm told that these days the region's artisans wouldn't want to work in Ceuta for love or money. This suggests that there's now sufficiently constant socioeconomic activity within the country's borders, and that the fragments of the national territory still occupied by Spain are no longer the economic magnets they once were. What this might mean for the elections is that new issues are coming to the fore at the level of domestic politics.

Meanwhile I note that the city of Tetouan has changed considerably. This sprawling provincial capital exerts a sizeable influence over the entire Rif. Its land base extends towards the country's east, and it values its old relations with that region and its counterpart in Morocco's western reaches. These days, the one-time capital of the Spanish Protectorate plays important administrative and military roles in the country's government, and houses the State's strategic apparatus. Multiple conurbations extend from Tetouan towards the Mediterranean coast, notably via Marfil. The urban surface area has more or less doubled in size, despite the limits imposed by the mountainous zone of Djebal Darsa . . . Recently, the city has begun to climb up its slopes, although its spread has been slowed down in the flood-prone alluvial plain of Oued Martil . . .

Numerous shantytowns have sprung up and a sizeable portion of the city's business is bound up with the contraband economy. Tetouan's economy is informal by definition. The city is itself 'informal'. Commercial activity and services, for which the city serves as regional centre, remain relatively strong. Among other functions, Tetouan supplies regional markets (even ones located farther away than Chefchaouen), sells wholesale to the souks of its neighbouring peninsula and mountain, and takes in agricultural products from the whole northern zone.

Return to Tangiers. On 17th August, on my way back from Rabat, I head into town. I've got a meeting with A.Z., a young engineer who's active in a movement that claims to be on the Left. Our discussion focuses on the enormous sums of money that are disbursed for dubious reasons during the election season as well as on the elections themselves. This young agronomist ran a newspaper which he then transformed into a publishing house. He also directs a theatre company. I admire his erudition and his open-mindedness.

Nothing is going on insofar as the elections are concerned, he tells me curtly. They lack the vibrant and invigorating atmosphere of election time in truly democratic countries . . . He dishes out the same remarks and arguments I've heard everywhere else.

From the 19th to the 20th August, I plan to spend the Anniversary of the Revolution of the King and the People[38] in Tetouan. Curiously, at 9.30 a.m. on this public holiday, the centre of Tangiers is nearly deserted. Nevertheless, shortly after we arrive the city begins to stir. In the cafe I've frequented for decades every time I've been here, the waiter seems overwhelmed. He waits on customers in a pell-mell manner, and even serves people who entered the cafe long after I sat down at my table and began my long wait for him to take my order. Although I have it out with him, I'm unhappy with the outcome of our exchange and decide to change cafes. I think my jumpiness can be explained by the toll that working as an observer is beginning to take on me. The effort that goes into getting a feel of the country's political pulse at this particular moment has, I think, made me particularly jittery. I can usually contain any aggressive feelings that might well up inside me, yet these days I occasionally let go and give them free rein.

On the A-road I take subsequently, I notice a new section of roadway under construction. In the past, the old network of motorways wasn't too bad, but it failed to meet the new demand. Moreover, the old roads weren't too comfortable and in some places were even dangerous. Their improvement is definitely a promising sign of progress and of the emergence of a new order of things in the region. A memo from the National Motorway Authority publicizes the large-scale construction projects under way: 'The stretch of road that links the Rabat–Tangiers motorway with the Tangiers–Tetouan A-Road was opened on July 28th, 2007. This section, which will eventually form part of the future motorway between *Tangiers-Port* and *Tanger-Med*, is 23 km long.'[39] It offers travellers who want to get to the Tangiers–Tetouan A-Road a safer and faster alternative. Moreover, it allows readier access to the industrial zone east of Tangiers while simultaneously helping drivers avoid having to cross the city's chaotic and poorly administered centre . . .

I head quickly to the beach in the middle of Mdiq to snatch a few moments of pleasure from its wonderfully azure and pellucid waters before I pursue my enquiries in the medina, which is where I've arranged to meet most of the people I want to talk to on this visit.

Clearly, smuggling, temporary leisure activities and many other summertime pursuits exert a strong effect on the life of the medina. They impede visitors from getting to know Tetouan in depth: its culture, its arts, its social fabric, its history, its way of life . . . Nevertheless, now that I've got myself stuck there, I see that the city is home to one of the most authentic of all medinas, with its warren of workshops and its hundreds of officially registered artisans. The place is abuzz with commercial activity and services . . .

On this 21st August, I wake up early ... I work on organizing my notes for a good two hours before I head out to my meeting at the corner cafe located a few steps away from where I'm staying, on one of Tetouan's principal main roads which runs through the Safir quarter, an uptown spot in the city's new urban fabric. I'm here to meet with an old Tetouani comrade, who grew up in the city and who's supposed to lead me into its depths. When I arrive, I discover him waiting for me.

We've decided to visit the district that's home to and named after the well-known Mazouak mosque and that we'll take a taxi there. Although he asks us whether it might not be preferable to take the upper route and obtains our assent, the driver takes the mountain road that leads to the quarter. He then nonchalantly takes Safir Avenue, which suddenly forks onto the street where the National Education Regional Academy is located, and where I held various opening ceremonies and numerous meetings when I was the minister of secondary and technical education. Now I pass in front of that building as though I'd never known it. Farther along there's a cemetery that I also know well. I once walked along this route when the father of one of our colleagues (who's since switched political allegiances) died. Perhaps my colleague no longer works there either.

In any case, now I wonder whether it wasn't unreasonable of us to cover this long route on foot. At the time, I wouldn't have understood what heading up towards the heights that overlook the city entailed. Now, the taxi is climbing the hill laboriously, so much so that I feel as though it's scaling the

mountain's summit. Moments later, we suddenly find ourselves in a rooftop position that looks out over the city. Never
before have I seen Tetouan panoramically spread out before
me from such an exceptional elevation. At that moment it
seems as though the city doesn't consist solely of a medina, a
colonial quarter, a jumble of variegated districts, suburbs and
countless housing estates. Instead, our vantage point reveals
strikingly dense concentrations of human habitation and
imposingly large communities fanning out hither and thither
... After taking in this unsuspected view, we set out on the
return journey which entails descending into the city down a
very steep slope. We pass through several streets which all
seem as though they belong in the heart of Tetouan. Along
the mountainside, a veritable city within a city spreads itself
out before us ...

We descend into the city proper and take a long road that
crosses the famous quarter of the Mazouak mosque. We cut
through the area diagonally and climb up to the top of one
of the heights that make up the district. Enormous fields
strewn with plastic bags of all colours meet our gaze. We see
a huge rubbish dump located just a few feet away from a
group of dwellings, right in front of their windows. Not far
from the dump there's a fountain with two taps that's been
erected to supply water to houses that haven't yet been connected to the municipal main. (That the main doesn't extend
to all homes is proof that this part of the quarter hasn't yet
shed its illicit status.) In contrast, the electricity supply seems
to be available to all the residents, even though few public
transmission lines can be seen. Most of the residences here
use septic tanks. As is the case throughout the country, what

we see here is evidence of ordinary lives being played out in licit or semi-licit informal settlements. Thus, after crossing a kind of frontier, a demarcation line, or, rather, a no man's land of sorts, a boundary beyond which households are dispersed across a zone that's poorly served by the city's infrastructure, we seem to enter a distinct and separate world.

On the way back, however, we're in for a big surprise. I thought we'd strayed far from the centre. Yet the city's topography is such that by taking a small fork in the road we once again end up in the modern heart of Tetouan. In fact, from where we'd just been, one could readily dispense with a taxi and get to the city centre on foot. A mere fifteen minutes is all it would take to end up a few feet away from the major avenues. I don't know why, but a very pleasant feeling sweeps over me when I discover that this other route takes you to the centre in no time. In travelling along the road I'd taken earlier, I'd had the impression that we were crossing over to another universe.

Crews from international television channels have filmed documentaries in the neighbourhood that houses the M. mosque. Pieces filed by foreign journalists emphasize the more sensational aspects of the lives of young people from these sorts of neighbourhoods who've ended up becoming terrorists ... They exaggerate facts that might interest readers in Madrid or New York, London or Paris, and maybe elsewhere as well. The people I meet with talk to me about these exaggerations which have become part and parcel of the global media circus of our times. Consciously or unconsciously, journalists of all ages who seek to stamp their style on their profession by penning rather inflammatory articles are fanning the flames of Islamophobia and xenophobia that are spreading like wildfire across the Western world.

'The notion that this neighbourhood produces suicide bombers is a short-lived myth. A number of channels toyed with this theory. But this city isn't Casablanca. Why do I say it's different? Well, take Lamrani, for instance, one of the bombers who people talked about a lot, and whom I knew. Initially he was totally lacking in character. It was later on in life that he changed . . .' Behind such stories one can discern the influence of a mixture of local Islamism, of Al Jazeera news bulletins, and of 'pariah culture' (*kif* smoking and dealing, smuggling, petty crime . . .)

Nevertheless, the neighbourhood does have a particular sort of character. Why is it that the despair that one finds in some of its streets seems to express itself much more strongly here than elsewhere, to the point that some of its inhabitants resort to political violence? And yet in some respects the neighbourhood couldn't be more ordinary. It resembles dozens of other such all over the country in which I've once again spent time this summer, which nevertheless don't yield up young men with such profiles. Nothing in particular makes it stand out, unless it be the fact that it was originally an informal settlement and that it still retains a hint of the illicitness associated with its founding. If anything, it's a bit cleaner than similar neighbourhoods, and its families and local authorities are clearly concerned with keeping things hygienic and orderly. A certain concern for order is noticeable. In fact, while walking around I noticed a privately owned garage in which the authorities were distributing voting cards . . .

Altogether, I've counted a score of mosques. What real needs are met by the desire to build so many places of worship? What we're talking about here is a neighbourhood that's a self-enclosed and self-sufficient world, with its visible and hidden economies, its communications network, its souks, its customs, its architecture . . .

When the Spaniards controlled Tetouan, they built single-storey homes, simple street-level constructions with semi-circular roofs of corrugated metal . . . These old buildings from the colonial period still stand, as does the cinema from that era, though it's no longer in use . . . This closed building seems strangely solitary even though it's surrounded by well-frequented cybercafes and phone shops, as well as a few tiny amusement arcades . . .

In this neighbourhood, ideological education is principally the bailiwick of two mosques. Community facilities may leave a lot to be desired, but their paucity doesn't amount to extreme poverty. Compared to that of numerous neighbourhoods in comparable communities, such penury as one finds here seems almost neat and tidy. What's dangerous about it is that, socially speaking, it seems to be situated in an intermediate zone, wedged between the middle classes on the one hand and the radically underprivileged sectors of Tetouani society on the other . . . It's quite clear that criminal elements as well as oppositional currents of diverse stripes can be readily take advantage of this social stratum and its location . . .

The Left is no longer a presence in the neighbourhood, whose social structure speaks volumes about the surrounding culture and its character: male and female workers in the industrial estate, women who live alone, soldiers and auxiliary forces ... I say the Left has no presence here even though the district has always legally voted for a socialist deputy. This fellow has always been an elected city councillor, even though he's moved from the Mazouak neighbourhood to the Safir quarter with which the former borders but which nonetheless lies outside the ward. This upstaging of the Left by political Islamism is a relatively novel phenomenon, in which the former keeps losing ground even while it maintains a token presence in the neighbourhood, at arm's length from its rival. At present, the neighbourhood's Islamist groupings seem to exert full control over it.

It's significant that the district underwent a growth spurt in the 1980s, the decade during which the drug trade mushroomed. One can find all kinds of drugs here: *pastillas*,[40] *qarqoubi*,[41] hashish, heroin, cocaine and synthetics imported from China. I'm told that here the goods aren't at all expensive: 20 dirhams, as opposed to twice that price in Tangiers ...

In the neighbourhood there's as much small-time crime as there is political activity. There's little visible police presence, even though I keep being told that there's an army of informers discreetly at work ... During the events of 1984, the neighbourhood's youth, its unemployed workers and its secondary-school students protested against the symbols of the established order and those who profit from them ... Informers and collaborators, social unrest, muddled subversion, perhaps the revolution, these are the everyday preserve of places such as this one.

At day's end, I meet up with the young man from ATTAC[42] with whom I'd briefly spoken in the morning in the Mazouak mosque neighbourhood ... He's made a point of ensuring that we meet after work in the centre of the modern part of the city, far from the neighbourhood. He didn't want to be seen with strangers. Social pressure is strong where he's from. 'I was born here. My life is bound up with the neighbourhood's. I don't want to be suspected of anything.' Talking to him isn't going to help unravel the ostensible mysteries of a tense urban zone. But meeting him allows me to establish a connection with someone who's aware of the issues and the challenges they pose. In any case, the conversation doesn't last long. The observations I make in my notebook are similar to those I've recorded around the country. My interlocutor has nothing to add to what I saw inscribed on the neighbourhood's streets this morning, or to what I noticed on every visage I scrutinized, every house I saw or in all the eyes I met. I've quoted the following remark in my notes, but can't identify its author: 'One can read appearances like one can read words, and, among all appearances, the human face is perhaps the most unfathomable of texts.'

On this 28th August, I head to the airport. I'm going to Beirut to take part in a colloquium once again. Shortly after my arrival, I learn via Al Jazeera of the demise of Driss Basri, the former minister of the interior who played a key role in Moroccan affairs since at least the 1970s and who, despite himself, continued to define the meaning of 'political correctness' in the post–Hassan II years. Nowadays in politics, everything that's looked upon as a good thing is defined in opposition to the former minister's conduct. I don't know why, but at this precise moment the memory of an exchange between us comes back to me forcefully. This is what he told me: 'I envy you, Abdallah, because you can walk around freely and meet whoever you like wherever you like. Do you realize how lucky you are?' Driss Basri has at last been freed from his role.

9.
MARRAKECH

The elections are no more than a few days away. Time is flying by. There are a good number of places I haven't yet set foot in and this distresses me. I hate to leave a task unfinished.

I get a phone call from an acquaintance in Marrakech who always goes through the same old routine of acting as though he's completely disillusioned with politics as it's practised among us. He acts as if he's seen and heard it all and as if he's finally had enough but then stands for election every time. He tells me that we shouldn't look to the upcoming elections for signs of authentic political projects, that they lack the atmosphere one finds at election time in genuine democracies. Instead, he claims, what we have here is a competition among very rich people, a contest between affluent business people from different localities who aspire to hold public office . . .

I'm told that in Marrakech (and I don't doubt that this is as true here as it is elsewhere) the political parties, even the national democratic parties (by which I mean those that haven't been 'fabricated' by the administration with a view to exerting even greater control over the political scene) have nearly all been fielding candidates who for the most part come from other political formations . . . Even those who were born into their respective parties are themselves hostages to their own organizations. A battle is brewing among individuals who will enter into alliances in order to form a government. These are the same people who've been standing for election for the past forty years . . .

In any case, it's time for me to go see what's going on in the Ochre City[43] so I set out early on the road to Marrakech. For the traveller who's coming down to the city from Rabat, Marrakech's influence can already be felt upon crossing the Oum Rbiâa River Valley. The region's distinctive features extend to the base of the Atlas Mountains and, on the other side, are to be found between the Tadla region in the centre of the country to Essaouira on the coast. I've long been intrigued by the relationship between Marrakech and the Haouz region to its immediate south-east, which was popularized by Paul Pascon's thesis,[44] which I'd read much before I got to know the Red City and its environs from up close, and even before I'd begun to travel in earnest and try my hand at writing . . .

From the road that leads to Marrakech, the city appears densely populated. On the way there, I pass by a large number of different landscapes in succession: low massifs, basins, stretches of arid, treeless earth, irrigated gullies in bright green tones, densely cultivated rural areas . . .

The rhythm of my visits to the region have never allowed me sufficient time to experience its distinctive climatic conditions. They say that, in general, conditions are harsh, that the climate changes from one year to the next, that drought-stricken zones are spreading everywhere. In any case, when I enter the region's spaces in late August, the temperature is soaring.

One senses that there was a time when there were considerable amounts of water available, as the region's great variety of water-retention structures seem to attest: *seguias*,[45] *khettaras*,[46] springs tapped on the left bank of the Tensift river, traditional wells, modern dams, motor pumps, water tankers . . .

Those who think strategically about the city's present and future devote more time to pondering the limits of the water supply than they do worrying about anything else. Large-scale works appear all along the route, as well as farmlands that decrease in size in proportion to the diminishing possibilities for irrigation. Farther away, in the hinterland where water is scarce, nature's harshness is even more in evidence.

Founded by Yousseff Ben Tachfine, the first sultan of the Almoravid Dynasty,[47] Marrakech still shows signs of its Saharan origins and ambitions. The different dynasties which succeeded one another were all oriented towards the rest of the African continent. Almoravids, Almohades[48] and, above all, Saadians[49] attempted to turn the city's location to their advantage. The record of their rule is marked by rupture, destruction and reconstruction . . .

Marrakech's population has thus far enjoyed continuous growth. The city attracts people to it by virtue of its status as the Haouz's workshop and as an important labour market. It's never shed its character as a large urban marketplace. Several urban centres make up the heart of the city but one effect of this concentration is to stifle the hinterland and subject it to its economic hegemony. Marrakech consumes large quantities of rural products and raw materials ... Sometimes, the city is compared to an enlarged head attached to a withered body. In any case, the city encourages familiarity with its ways. It's at once a reception centre, a manufacturing hub and a distribution depot for finished artisanal products. It also attracts rural artisans, wholesalers and retailers and weekly souks from a large swath of the south.

The region's entire commercial life is channelled via Marrakech. According to a number of analyses, this prevents the emergence of commuter towns. Green belts brimming with market gardens, dairy cowsheds and large farms spread out around the city. It's clear that traditional ways survive, especially in relation to farming. There seems to be quite a bit of traffic on the roads, especially those that lead to the Atlas Mountains, the city and province of El Kelaâ des Sraghna, Tadla ...

The floodplain and the *dir* look like completely different domains. Along the road, tree-filled landscapes and compact, intensely cultivated orange and almond groves extend as far as the eye can see ... Nevertheless, the terrain is fragmented, punctuated by dense human settlement and a sprawling network of open irrigation ducts (seguias) ... One gets the impression that barley is the dominant crop here, and that the landscape is only sparsely populated with fruit trees ... Suddenly, however, there appears the fertile orchard of the Targa zone. And in the other direction, a rare instance of a palm grove outside the country's Saharan region ...

Marrakech's surroundings are as captivating as the city itself. The latter has expanded around the medina, one of the largest in the whole of Maghreb and a magnet for people from the countryside, urban dwellers and tourists alike. In its expansion, Marrakech hasn't followed a single pattern of urban development. Rather, it's mushroomed around an array of differentiated urban clusters, of which some extend into the outskirts or the suburbs . . .

Marrakech's urban core is formed by the medina's artisanal and commercial sections, from Jamaâ El Fna to the gates of Bab Doukkala and Bab El Khémis. This part of the city is much sought after by foreign investors who transform old homes and riads into sumptuous dwellings or guesthouses. Hundreds of these transformations take place every year.

A bit farther away, we find the Sidi Youssef Ben Ali quarter, a part of the city that consists of formerly periurban zones that have in effect become extensions of the medina where people uprooted from the rural areas congregate. We also find douars, at first of a makeshift sort but then transformed into urban districts that have since been restructured and integrated into the city proper.

Marrakech is also in part a tourist town. The portions of the city that tourists frequent gleam like carefully polished precious stones. Within their bounds we find hotels, the city's modern hub, an extension of the old colonial quarter and tertiary activities, Gueliz, the Hivernage district and the Koutoubia minaret.[50] The hotel industry, specialist bazaars, car-rental agencies, guide services and coach companies provide plenty of employment. Marrakech's attractiveness as a world-renowned destination has served to disconnect the touristy parts of town from the rest of the city . . .

At the edge of the old colonial *ville*, the industrial and working-class quarter is hemmed in by an infrastructural belt of garages, factories and warehouses and other industrial developments on the road to Safi in the north-west. They say that nowadays industrial activity is stagnant, especially in the food-processing industry, with the available employment being mostly seasonal in nature, along with whatever jobs cement works, commerce and artisanal workshops may provide.

On another level, we've got the working-class douars of Tziki, Mhamid. Properly speaking, there are no shantytowns in Marrakech. On the other hand, middle-class Marrakech includes pockets of well-to-do households as well as former douars that have been increasingly regularized, for instance, the Amerchich neighbourhood or the recent and enormous development of Al Massira.

Finally, there is a vast discontinuous zone which corresponds to the palm grove and which includes luxury residences, hotel complexes, vast subdivisions and a not-very-heavily built-up area, the whole of which forms a large arc of a circle which connects to the Fez road. An immense stretch of garden spaces traverses the entirety of the city.

Marrakech seems open to the surrounding countryside. Indeed, the city consumes virtually its entire vicinity, even though its business-activity catchment area would appear to be well delimited. Middle-class transplants from Casablanca and Agadir have relocated to the region to establish farms, small hotels and secondary homes in the approaches to the city.

In contrast to Fez, which enjoys close links with its hinterland, Marrakech maintains a kind of estranged relationship with its suburbs. What is noticeable in just about all the places I've visited is once again confirmed here in Marrakech—the country's political terrain is characterized by a pronounced Balkanization that is symptomatic of its diversity. At the same time, the overall capacity of the political parties to integrate citizens into their ranks seems reduced. This is far from being an exclusively Marrakechi problem, but, rather, a reflection of what's taking place virtually all across the land. Everywhere, Marrakech included, the elections are casting light on how localized the nation's communities are. By the same token, they're revealing that there's little discussion of essential national questions between politicians and the different social strata.

The problem of Balkanization leads one to wonder about the centrality of the elections and the role of the parliamentary system in the political arena. Perceptions of the place and role of Parliament seem negative. The rush to engage in new forms of cheating—circumvention of the law, misuse of funds, abuse of influence, undue use of public resources—has generated increasing loss of confidence in Parliament's character and function and further degrades its image.

The number of political parties has been a 'source of concern' since the 1993 elections. People complained that there were too many. The 2005 Law of Parties was intended to change the nature of relations between the establishment and the political parties. It sought to reorganize the political field by creating major political forces and by checking the propensity for creating political parties on the slightest pretext . . .

I maintain that in a country like ours, where the least one can say is that for several decades now elections have generally been marked by suspiciousness, by lack of transparency, by manoeuvring and by vote-rigging, it would have been advisable to open up the political arena by allowing other parties to see the light of day. Doing so would have helped the tendencies that structure Moroccan society find better expression. Afterwards, the free play of politics would have decided who should stay in the game and who ought to bow out . . .

By pure chance, I can also do here what I've been able to do elsewhere. By adding several categories to my schema, I can complete my typology of candidates who can be dubbed 'independent'. There are those, for instance, who want to come across as being apolitical but who could be construed as political in a certain sense. Or there are those who claim to align themselves with a higher politics, a politics 'above the party-political fray'. Lack of political engagement, which is often an issue around the country, raises questions about security in those places where politicians forget that they're in charge of the machinery which guarantees the preservation of the established order. But apolitical positions also reveal a confusion between the local and the national. With regard to the future, we can't rule out a scenario that seems just as possible as the possibility of continued lack of engagement: an eventual awakening to politics as challenges are taken up. The dawning of political awareness often seems to come about when certain problems present themselves.

In Marrakech, I notice the ideological character of the campaign carried out by certain political parties, especially left-wing ones. The increasing Americanization of campaigning methods and means, the increasingly dominant use of the mass media ... none of this manages to diminish the strongly traditionalist tenor of elections in Morocco, in which candidates frequently invoke both their Sharifian credentials[51] and 'El Aâr'. Traditionalism also expresses itself in other ways, such as the organization of large celebrations, the limits imposed on different sources of information, the enormous obstacles that lie in the way of mobilization in rural areas, as well as a revealing phenomenon: weak attendance at meetings and the very limited mobilizing capacity of political organizations ... Customary affiliations, personal relations, client networks, the 'useful' vote in a context of new property rights ... all of these things seem to count for more than political convictions. This tendency is only reinforced by the fact that the culture of voting isn't deeply anchored. Other factors also play into this situation, for instance, the feeble rate of voter registration, the elevated level of non-participation and the high number of annulled ballots over the course of all the previous elections. The reasons for the degree of demobilization seem to vary from election to election. It could be argued that the function of the elections is to designate the persons responsible for executing whatever policies are set by the supreme representative. From this standpoint, the purpose of the elections is not to obtain a governing majority—with the king still serving as head of state—but simply to designate the nation's representatives. Thus, the elections would seem to serve as a means for entrenching the legitimacy of the central authority. There can be no question, therefore, of the elections serving to attenuate the latter's hegemony.

In crossing Ben Guérir in the middle of the day, I once again notice the absence of any sign of the elections. During a wonderful journey I took in the region with Samir Amin,[52] a trip that remains indelibly imprinted in my memory, I remember that, for reasons that escape me, he called it 'Kansas City'. Might it be its horse-drawn carriages and the continuous hustle and bustle of its centre that lend the city the appearance of a 'cow town'? Or could it be the low houses ranged alongside the main road and its air of being a large market town?

I'm told that at this precise moment in time a good number of people I've got to know in politics during the last two decades are in Ben Guérir to pay obeisance to the official whom I discussed earlier in this travelogue, who after resigning became, by force of circumstance, the favourite candidate of this ward. The waiter at the cafe-restaurant on the city's main road, who's known me for years, tells me all about this high-flying group of people who've come from Rabat, from Casablanca, from other cities, from all over the country's interior as well as abroad to seek an audience with, and offer their services to, the erstwhile senior official. The waiter says, 'So and so is here, and so is so and so . . . you know, even whatshisname is in town.' And so on . . .

10.
THE SOUSS

My travelling companion in these immense spaces comes across as a businessman through and through. He's in a constant state of alertness, constantly occupied and preoccupied and always engaged in the only worthwhile activity he knows, viz., making money. His workshops are located both in and on the outskirts of Agadir. First, we drive together from Marrakech to the capital of the Souss region. He'd already told me, on several different occasions, the story of how he made a fortune. He started out selling postcards for a national distributor of newspapers and books. Then one day he decided to work for himself. Specializing in the marketing of paints, cleaning products and products for domestic use, he later started manufacturing them.

As a politician, he'd already been fielded as a candidate for right-wing and centre parties in successive previous elections, if, that is, terms such as 'right' and 'centre' can be said to have a meaning in the specific context of the Souss region. We talk about the highly visible public-works projects we see being implemented all around us: road repairs, the creation of access to drinking water, the installation of basic facilities . . . we see these works being undertaken all along the route, as if miraculously speeded up during this period prior to the popular vote . . .

We spend much of our time discussing and analysing the impact of the elections in the rural areas. What are the main perspectives that are being brought to bear upon them? What about them stands out? What can we hypothesize about them? I have to say that, by the time we reach the Souss, I'm beginning to feel something like saturation with regard to the elections. The observations I make and the conclusions I reach here don't seem to differ much from those I've made and reached elsewhere.

In any case, I notice that, in these parts, foreigners rent or purchase as much land as they like, both along the coast (between Oued Massa and Oued Souss) and in the interior. In fact, so much foreign capital has been invested in the region that prices have climbed very high, so high that they're beginning to lie beyond the reach of the locals, land suddenly having attained a hitherto unimaginable value.

What's happening these days with respect to 'Soussi capitalism'? The regional personalities who have made their mark at the national level continue to journey along their chosen paths to success. Satisfied in their palatial country homes, they've amassed empires of vegetables, grain, oil, petrol, textiles and industrial products. In the Souss, several sectors (and several fortunes) have acquired a strategic significance. For instance, food processing and packaging are major activities in this fruit- and citrus-growing paradise. Furthermore, the number of argan-oil cooperatives has increased considerably, and their conditions of cultivation and production—as well as their earnings—seem to have improved. Everywhere we go, we're told that the lack of access to water is a major concern. Numerous reservoirs and water tables seem to have run dry.

While riches pile up for some, immiseration becomes the norm for others. There's a great deal of poverty throughout the zone and internal migration is in full swing. People come here from all over the country to work in agriculture. They come here from such places as Chiadmas, Khénifra, Ouerzazate, Abdas, Doukkalas. At Khmiss Bani Amir, it seems as though the map of Morocco has been replicated: Douar Lhmer, Douar el Arab, Douar Taoss, etc. I'm told that prostitution is practised on a large scale, even in the formerly pious country-side. Are those who intone the refrain, 'the onetime land of Siba is now the country of SIDA (AIDS)'? really overstating things or are they being ironic?[53]

The large numbers of factories that have cropped up in the region have led to a massive influx of men and women from other parts of the country, and sexual relations outside marriage have now become an ordinary feature of the social landscape. People speak of the region's downward spiral in matters of sexuality, prompted as much by the problems workers face (whether they be migrants or not) as by the fairly enormous influx of tourists.

Hence the tendency among locals to preach at all and sundry. (Curiously, the part of the Souss that's deemed the most amoral is that in which irrigation is increasingly becoming a challenge.) The most conservative of local voices describe a descent into hell. Rural delinquency is also part of the picture. The rustling of livestock is widespread.

New habits have taken root in the Souss and a novel culture has emerged. As regards births, deaths, celebrations, marriage, divorce or modes of mourning, the way things are done has changed. There's no doubt that a transformation of the traditional way of life—indeed, a sea-change in values—is taking place here. From now on, the Souss interior will be subjected to the influence of urban ways of living. For instance, in the past everybody just showed up at the celebrations organized by the region's families. Nowadays, they come by invitation only: time is in much shorter supply than before. Previously, guests dined on dishes served up by the hosts: these days they eat meals prepared by caterers ... Doubtless, these sorts of changes are analogous to those we're seeing in the rest of the country, which make sense and are predictable, but, although change may be the norm everywhere, its content differs from region to region.

The landscape has also changed. Infrastructure and facilities have multiplied and new buildings are sprouting up everywhere, a sign of the establishment of new services: community clinics, hospitals, primary and secondary schools, the local offices of different ministries, the headquarters of various organizations, banks, chemists and the people who are part of all that ... Moreover, along the coast, campsites burgeon on erstwhile virgin beaches. Projected large-scale public works will swallow up whole stretches of coastline.

A local man makes the following observation: 'Here in the countryside, at the close of day, we used to sit down on the terrace and gaze at the horizon while sipping a cup of tea. In the past, the landscape stretched out before us endlessly, and nothing obstructed the view. Nowadays, the entire region is covered with all sorts of structures.'

(Young) women's liberation seems to be gaining ground here. Soussi women used to be conservative, which doesn't mean that the region was fundamentalist. Women's clothes have changed and women no longer give birth at home. Instead they do so at the community clinic or at the hospital ... Although they may not be very apparent, these are major changes.

For all the transformations that it's undergoing, the Souss is still characterized by a very special sort of conviviality, signalled in part by the abundance of grilled food, fruit, doughnuts and mint tea. The aroma of the little tagines of Aourir is still appetizing and a profound sense of naturalness emanates from the region's people and places. This unaffected character is part of everyday life in the Souss's large urban centres, such as Inezgane, Aït Melloul, Ben Serghaou, with their residential and commercial areas, their workspaces and even their leisure spots. Beyond the debates over the status of Amazigh culture, the towns and cities of the Souss are melting pots in which the language of an entire people is used as a means of communication. These areas can be characterized as matrices for Morocco's integration. And yet, despite the specificity of nationwide continuities, these districts and towns resemble Derb Ghallef[54] in the 1960s and 70s: dense population centres, middle-class demographic profiles, national-poverty statistics, working-class restaurants that the lower middle classes can afford, a melting pot with garish colours and shrill sounds as dominant features of the social landscape, lots of green and red ... In these sorts of spaces, one has a good chance of seeing evidence of what we might call social cohesion ...

Agadir is also the capital of a certain strain within the Amazigh movement, which was reorganized after the well-known summer school held in the city in 1981, where a call was made for unity in diversity. The meetings drew many young people and cadres and became the indispensable reference point for the Amazigh movement in all its variety. Other associations also emerged and thus were many young members and cadres in the region who were trained, a fact that benefitted the central State . . .

In terms of financial and cultural support, the Souss remains the backbone of the Amazigh movement. The most active members of the movement remain those who come from the Souss rather than their counterparts in the Rif. For the most part, they are on the political Left, although Imazighen of Islamist tendencies aren't rare either.

All these folks now are active in the Royal Institute of Amazigh Culture.[55] In contrast to the situation in Nador, here in this summer of 2007 the idea of regional autonomy doesn't seem to have caught on. In the Souss, we're in the heart of the country and at the centre of the tendency towards national integration, a process which seems as advanced as it is irresistible. More than elsewhere, here one feels strongly a bolstering of the bonds of nation, society and identity. The Souss is one of the great matrices of Moroccanness. One of its particularities is that it captures equally well the specificity and the diversity that make up the nation's cohesion. The country is changing and its problems are heterogeneous. Each region contains its fair share of paradoxes, some of which are region-specific and others which are shared with other parts of the country. For instance, a paradoxically fragile yet powerful sense of irreducible Moroccanness, historical memory, or lands, customs and practices. Each region has a geostrategic dimension and serves as mould for the armed forces, the administrative machinery and the ideological apparatus of the State . . .

Two facts stand out forcefully: on the one hand, many activists in the Souss's Amazigh movement have their roots in left-wing politics. On the other, under Soussi skies, the causes of Arab unity and of Islam have always created strong bonds and rested on firm foundations. Several facts attest to the truth of this claim: for instance, the numerous translations of key Islamic texts that are widely available here—including that of the Quran itself—the region's many mosques, the very important networks of traditional schools and the high level of engagement with, or sympathy for, all of the great Arab causes. Here in Agadir, I've participated in very important meetings devoted to the unity of the Maghreb and the Arab world, to the question of Palestine, to solidarity with Iraq when it was attacked by Western armies and their allies . . . In contrast to the radicalism that one finds in the Atlas Mountains, here one gets a sense of the distinctively balanced character of Soussi culture.

At this stage of my journey, I can't help but summarize my observations. Agadir is taking off in every sense. One can feel it flourishing. Soon its spread along the coast will stabilize itself. There, at least, the city's limits are clear. Nevertheless, it's possible that it'll continue to spread towards the north and the south . . . Several urban patches are breaking away from the city. For instance, the tourist area—one of whose characteristics is that it lacks a mosque. The taxi driver tells me: 'The people who come here pray on Sundays.' In the modern part of the city, which was built during the colonial period, there's nothing worthier of note than the official buildings (local authority, *wilaya*,[56] State Bank, the post office ...). And then there's the endless Agadir of multiple peripheral districts, plus a belt of urban centres and market towns ... I should note that, when the electoral season is officially launched, those who talk to me about the elections point out that there are few new candidates ...

All of the city's cultural life is organized around the importation of ideas and of speakers and performers. National and international institutions, foundations, associations and the country's major political, economic, social and cultural organizations come here to hold their activities. Comparatively speaking, Agadir gets very little from the interior, aside from folklore for tourists.

11.

THE DEEP SOUTH
(WESTERN SAHARA)

I head down to the Saharan region[57] to learn more about the major issues at stake there. The conditions of observation throughout the Saharan territory are always different from those one finds elsewhere. What is political life like in the region under the conditions we've been examining? How are the season's electoral campaigns unfolding there?

Altogether, these immense expanses of land constitute the country's crucial fourth major zone, not just because of the central role it played in the Sahelian kingdoms throughout history but also because of its present realities and doubtless because of its future as well. Every time I traverse the Saharan region's flat immensities, I feel a great joy. This time around, the elections are almost a pretext to visit these parts. I love to immerse myself in the territory's arid flatness. I love to lose myself in its vastness which every so often is traversed by dry riverbeds and sunken spaces, by dunes and by invisible trails that crisscross the sands . . .

In recent years, there have been changes in the discourses and policies surrounding the question of the incorporation of the southern regions into the rest of the country.[58] In relation to the Western Sahara, internal issues are bound up with elements of international affairs, geopolitical and strategic matters blend with cultural ones, and the social and the sociological are mutually imbricated. An issue like the future of the Sahara ought to take centre place in public debate and in the elections ... Yet the same old arguments and rhetoric against our adversaries are trotted out, almost mechanically, in a manner that's utterly lacking in imagination or creative thought. This tired discourse in no way does justice to the changing realities of the Western Sahara.

In these parts, one often hears talk of frequent sandstorms. However, although I've spent long periods in the region's deserts at different times of the year and travelled across vast stretches of its landscapes, I've never experienced a sandstorm and wonder what it's like to live through one in the region's interior. Every aspect of life in these parts is affected by the lack of fresh water. People seem to live between surface sources of water and deep waters. To everybody's dismay, desertification is proceeding apace and the extant sandy area is permanently increasing. Yet the history books tell us that these lands weren't always quite so arid, not even during the period since Roman colonization ...

The Saharan territory consists of a sparsely inhabited interior and of coastal hubs that are experiencing continuous growth. It's rich in economic resources and activities that principally revolve around fishing, phosphates and tourism ... Considerable investments have been made in the region's development, and the State has expended large sums of money in building up its infrastructure with the aim of integrating more fully into the nation a territory that's subject to strong international pressures. Formerly nomadic, the

Western Sahara's population has become largely sedentary and urban, and developed new needs. The size of the urban population is growing ceaselessly. Different groups have settled in El-Aiún because of the armed conflict that lasted until 1991, but also because people have chosen to live in the city.

Every time I approach Smara, I remember the Tharaud brothers' travel narrative.[59] Whether they are coming from the north (Guelmine) or the west (El-Aiún), even at a fair distance from the city something in the air announces to travellers that they are entering a historical and cultural hub. This unique city of the interior exerts a strong fascination which is linked, among other things, to the *zaouïa Maa El Aïnine*.

Smara is undergoing sustained demographic growth. People settled in the city as a result of the armed conflict, at least until 1991. Essentially, the city lives off commerce which is quite lively. It seems that livestock farming, based on transhumance in search of nourishing routes for the flocks and herds, is also widely practised here . . .

The town has a clearly military function. By a strange coincidence, I have occasion to chat with the military commander of the garrison . . . He strikes me as an open-minded, hands-on and highly moral sort of person and the type of officer who is strikingly efficient in the face of adversity. Despite all the problems they have with the civilian population, his men's morale remains high . . . The commander takes me on a quick tour of the town, its main thoroughfares, its back alleys, its few cafes, the headquarters of the administration's decentralized services . . .

The night of the day of my arrival will be long. I gather with members of the local branch of our national association, that is to say, with comrades. We sit down on the floor in a large room and get comfortable by extending our entire bodies along the floor. The meeting is naturally informal but engaging. Impressive carpets have been unfurled for the occasion at the guesthouse where we're gathered. We all congregate around a large *mechoui*.[60] Young people, former prisoners and local elected representatives alike all cluster around an enormous and exceedingly well-stocked platter. Enjoying the limitless supply of tea, we introduce ourselves and then talk until very late in the evening about all manner of subjects, including, for instance, the forum's organizational problems and its activities at the local and national levels. Some of the attendees were present at the most recent summer school I'd organized in Tetouan back in mid-July.

We also talk about local politics which are apparently both constrained and suppressed by the question of the Sahara as understood in its wider regional context, that is to say, the western Saharan region of the African continent . . . Insofar as the elections are concerned, I'm told that the die is cast. Some of my interlocutors are returnees from the refugee camps in Tindouf.[61] They all have different things to say about exile, about being held in detention, about crossing borders, about arriving in Western Sahara, about the welcome they received there, about their attempts at adapting to novel realities, about rebelling, about their hopes and expectations . . .

A good number of my interlocutors linger over the famous five dossiers on which are based the debates between those who argue for the incorporation of the Western Sahara into the Moroccan state and those who advocate independence. Among the matters under debate: reparations for the victims of landmines, the recruitment of phosphate workers, the fate of those who were imprisoned for political reasons during the Years of Lead, the situation of unemployed university graduates . . . Everyone takes the elections seriously. But sometimes I get the impression that here the elections are construed as a mechanism for maintaining the dominant equilibrium among the region's tribes, which results in all sorts of underhandedness.

After I leave, I learn that our gathering and I have been the subjects of an investigation by the 'services', who wanted to know what was said during this all-night meeting. In particular, they wanted to know what I said. At first, I was upset by this mistrust towards somebody like me, an active proponent of the national cause, and, moreover, a former minister in the Alternance government.[62] A friend from El-Aiún, who's a municipal councillor here, an independent who's widely respected in the area, observes that, 'The fact that they come here to investigate a former official in their own government shows that they don't trust anybody. How will they regard the rest of us, especially when they know that many of us are former members of POLISARIO who have only rallied to the cause of Moroccan unity relatively late in the day?'[63] A little later, however, I conclude that their behaviour isn't really out of order in a State that claims to be well run. But one wishes that the 'services' in question had acted a bit more skilfully, discreetly and tactfully. In any case, I trust that in this sort of situation agents will file reports containing a true account of what was said, rather than distortions of the truth.

The sun is high up in the sky when we set out on the road to El-Aiún, at a distance of 201 km from us. As we journey westward, the landscape's immutability becomes more and more taxing. At every step of the way, all our vehicle's windows reveal the same scenes and ours is the only car on the roadway. However, every once in a while, enormous installations and heavy equipment loom out of the emptiness. At times too we witness the indescribable beauty of great heights in the midst of utterly flat surroundings. My travelling companion points out some of the places in which the national police have found sub-Saharan migrants, and even migrants from South Asia . . . How did Pakistanis and Sri Lankans manage to get here in their attempt to enter Europe via the Canary Islands?[64]

A short while later, the first buildings come into view. Has the city grown a bit too fast, I wonder? I'd already read somewhere that the surface area of El-Aiún has indeed expanded in the direction of Smara. Everything about the place—its proportions, its neighbourhoods, its urban layout, as well as the way its residents look at you, the gleam in their eyes, their mien—conveys the unmistakable impression that the city is the capital of its province and its region.

En route to El-Aiún, I glean from a variety of documents that major infrastructural developments include the linking up of the Western Sahara's urban centres to the national road network at several junctions, and the installation throughout the territory of seawater desalination plants. The picture is rendered more complete if it includes an increase in the number of groundwater drilling sites and sewage-treatment plants (the latter's deficiencies notwithstanding), along with the extension of the grid. In addition, seaports and airports are under construction. Moreover, social policies have not been left behind: for instance, the provision of public schooling and public-health facilities over the course of the past two decades has been nothing short of remarkable . . .

El-Aiún's lively demographic growth makes it the principal city of the South and considerable numbers of people have moved there. Research has established that more than two-thirds of these people are originally from the Southern Provinces.[65] Barely more than a third of them were born in El-Aiún itself, with the remainder hailing from neighbouring provinces of Tan Tan and Guelmine (13.6 per cent). Considerable numbers of residents (22.8 per cent) originally hail from the Northern Provinces.

Now, in the middle of the day, the visitor is struck by the number of people here. How to grasp the spirit of this metropolis? It's at once an oasis for nomads, a place that attracts civil servants and other public employees, a magnet for traders, shopkeepers, contractors and service providers. In El-Aiún, the informal sector has found one of its favourite locales.

On that note, I must draw attention to the economic diversification that characterizes the region's capital. For one thing, the city has developed a very particular sort of urban economy. A good percentage of the population is engaged in livestock farming, with more than 1,200 farmers living in the city. Several hundred herders and farmworkers accompany the herds. With their incessant coming and going between town and country and their armies of four-legged ruminants searching for grazing grounds, these herders are cause for worry. They give the appearance of an impressive strike force. I can't help but think that they might play a formidable role in the elections, in every electoral activity that requires mobilization and with regard to the various social movements ... Livestock farming lies at the heart of the city's economy.

But so do other activities, with the primary sector—fishing, mining and agriculture (around the perimeter of Foum El Oued)—occupying a prominent place. These days, primary-sector activities employ thousands of people, as does the tertiary sector with its 20,000 employees. Fish processing has also generated jobs. And to this list one must add large numbers of people employed by the army.

El-Aiún's growing population bespeaks a dynamic that seems to have taken hold of the city ever since its retrocession to the Moroccan State.[66] At times, the city gives the impression of being infrastructurally over-endowed. The State's dynamic intervention is the principal source of El-Aiún's major infrastructure: an airport, modern desalination and water-purification plants, two thermal power stations, a fast-increasing supply of domestic electricity ...

The State's intervention in the local economy is particularly noticeable in the housing sector, where it ranks as the principal developer and provider of accommodation, a role which, according to its critics, has brought to light the absence of a real property market subject to the laws of supply and demand. The existing housing stock doesn't seem terribly diversified, consisting as it does of blocks of flats of a middling sort, of cheap houses with a ground floor plus one, two or three more floors and of neighbourhoods with villas. In addition, there are houses modelled on northern dwellings but adapted to local circumstances by having separate pathways for the livestock ... There are also strangely shaped colonial structures, such as spherical constructions ... Finally, there are official buildings well endowed with diverse facilities ...

El-Aiún is not without its problems, most of which are linked to the desert environment in which it's ensconced. Lack of water remains an enormous problem. There are also problems which stem from the city's precipitous growth. Accommodation, for instance, is still in very short supply, and, after the urban fabric inherited from the colonial period became overcrowded, the first districts of substandard housing came into being as tent cities were transformed into shantytowns. Much dysfunction has flowed from that transformation. Inadequate sanitation constitutes one of the most crucial difficulties the city faces. In El-Aiún, much waste is disposed of in the open. The two days I spent discussing the state of the city have enabled me to take stock of its prospects.

We set out on the road to El Marsa in order to get a better sense of the haunting world of labour as well as of the material conditions of everyday life. In this conurbation, where it isn't easy to make a living, we see an impressive body of labourers hard at work. Here, where the provisions of the welfare state are rather scarce, the workers expend themselves simply in order to subsist. A formidable fleet of lorries drive up and down the region's roads. Paradoxically, and despite everything these roadways endured during the war years, the roads—like black lines traced on nearly white sand—still have a new and imposing air about them.

The port city of El Marsa exhibits all the problems that come with unbridled population growth and with uncontained urban sprawl, and which are characterized, in part, by inadequate infrastructure. At present, fish-processing plants discharge their effluent directly into the sea, as do tailings from nearby mines. Moreover, the town's housing stock seems unplanned, and is beset by administrative woes.

On the whole, the region's economic development seems to centre on its littoral, somewhat to the detriment of the interior. Initially, most infrastructure, service activities and fish processing were to be found in the old colonial port. The new port that's under construction should develop the fishing fleet's capacity, facilitate (via coastal navigation) commercial relations with northern ports and enable economic diversification.

I leave this factory zone with its proletarian quarters to spend the night in the conurbation of Foum El Oued. Given the industrial surroundings, my hotel's decor strikes me as incongruously nomadic, what with its murals of camels and camel drivers. Outside my room, the sea roars. I become aware of the town's character as a 'seaside resort', one of many such places all along the coast. As I gaze upon it, the place strikes me as indistinguishable from its sundry counterparts along the Atlantic coast.

I take the road that leads to Dakhla with the firm intention of fully experiencing the long distance to my destination *precisely as distance,* that is to say, as both an interval of space to be traversed and as the condition of travelling to a far-off point. I've already undertaken this road-trip on several occasions and look forward to undertaking both the outward-bound journey and the return home. Amid these lunar landscapes, the passage through dunes and wide stretches of sand amounts to a veritable crossing of the desert. When I examine my motivations, I realize that I traverse the desertscape not so much because I want to reach the town that lies on the other side of its expanses but because the traversal itself suffuses me with a sense of joy. My desert crossing is both literal and figurative: it entails a loss of bearings, a long period of solitude and a profound experience of silence.

Yet after a certain time has elapsed, one does eventually reach the town of Dakhla, administrative centre of another of the country's large regions. The town has been resettled in the wake of the armed conflict, even while rural municipalities have been administratively revived. Here too, the grouping of different people from the rural areas and the return of the original population from isolated places lacking in infrastructure have been heightened by the influx of fisherfolk, civil servants and employees working on contract for different government agencies. All of this translates into a demographic growth as notable as that of all the other urban centres of the Southern Provinces. Dakhla also suffers from problems with the housing stock and a notorious shortage of accommodation.

12.
MOROCCO'S MANY DIMENSIONS

It's already 20th September. The elections have taken place. The results are known and a new government is being formed. At no point in writing this travelogue have I been principally motivated by the desire to analyse the elections or to monitor the unfolding political process. From the outset, my principal motivation has been to provide an account of the political state of the nation ...

Once the elections are over, once their results have been tallied, once the first round of positions (e.g. prime minister, speaker of Parliament, chairman of various bodies, plus direct and indirect appointments ...) have been filled in, most likely by the same people who occupied them earlier, once the government has been formed, once Parliament is back in session, once everything is back to normal, what will the country's politics, economy and society be like? What will life *tout court* be like? Despite everything, the issue of understanding the place of the elections in the life of the country still strikes me as central, even if the elections themselves aren't of decisive importance.

It can be conceded that the popular vote functions as a kind of social safety valve. On occasion, they can serve as a release for pent-up tensions. They can also enable the redeployment of the relevant stakeholders and the redefinition of roles or their confirmation. Furthermore, they make possible the development of an economy that's peculiar to the elections themselves.

At certain moments in Morocco's recent history, elections have taken on a symbolic value, insofar as they capture the political stakes of the current phase. Two interrelated questions then arise. Might the significance of the elections have been overstated? And might stakeholders who demanded change been too quick to adjudge the elections as a watershed in the country's history since independence, simply because they took place under conditions of almost satisfactory transparency? A vision of the country that places primary emphasis on the significance of elections is wide of the mark. As a number of analysts observed, to overplay the importance of elections misses the point that what's important about them is that they breathe some momentum into political life and lead to a renewal of a sector of the elites. This sort of continuity comes with elections of a better quality.

To take in all of the country's elements: the autumnal breezes of Agadir and its environs, the sands of Foum El Oued, the polluted effluent of El Marsa and El-Aiún, the marginality of Larache and other port cities, the stench of the open-air refuse tips in the towns of the Western Sahara, the bizarrely shaped minaret that rises from the heart of town, the rural mosques of the Zaër country, the flies at Arekmane, the haughty mien of the bazaar merchants of Marrakech, the calm assurance of the vendors of Meknes and other such 'imperial cities', as the guidebooks call them, the infinite flexibility and tact of the traders of Fez, the radiant smile of the women who suddenly cross your path in one of Khenifra's back alleys, the floating airs of Azrou, the roving gaze of the people of the desert . . .

A side-note: one day, in a luxury hotel of a bygone Tripoli, Commander Jalloud, at the time Libya's second-in-command, discoursed in front of an audience of intellectuals from all the countries in the region. I had the impression that he was looking me straight in the eye. But upon changing position I noticed that he was staring at some other thing that I couldn't situate. When I mentioned this to a friend, he whispered, 'He's a man of the desert. He sees mirages wherever he goes.'

To have seen places, to have experienced them, to have regularly visited 120 localities across the length and breadth of the country *before* undertaking my most recent journey, to have visited each of them on at least a dozen occasions (and to have visited other sites less often, including places I passed through only once), to have eaten there, savoured their dishes, conversed, slept and dreamt . . . Does all of this render one better equipped to apprehend the country's distinctiveness? Does having contemplated the sun rise or the sun set in all of these places help one comprehend the world which they comprise?

The numerous changes that have taken place in all of these sites in spatial and infrastructural terms, in terms of the distribution of people and the deployment of their activities throughout the land, the evolution of social structures, all these realities are too diverse to allow for a coherent overview of the country. The responses that their realities elicit all seem different from one another. It necessarily follows that to fashion a project for the whole of Moroccan society is a difficult undertaking. It seems logical not to confuse the local with the national. Programmes pitched at too general a level come across as pro forma exercises. They give off a whiff of plagiarism, and are redolent of planning departments and politically correct expertise. It's not for their generality or their excessive insistence on specificity that I reproach them. Rather, it's for their dearth of engagement with conditions around the country as well as their lack of a vision of the society as a whole . . .

The month of Ramadan returns. Austere days succeed one another. One evening, after breaking the fast, I have a conversation with A.K. My project of visiting all the different parts of the country and to encounter their mundane realities and their myths, their lands and their localities, their little people and their elites, their traditions and their modern realities had from the outset turned on one principal idea: What, on the eve of our national elections, is the state of our nation? This hasn't been a matter of tallying votes and of crunching numbers. Rather, my project has entailed capturing the spirit of the moment in the hope that my grasp of present realities wouldn't miss the point.

In writing these pages, my only ambition has been to better understand and describe the situation around the country. I never intended to embark upon a literary or anthropological adventure with the grandiose aim of 'describing a situation with such veracity . . . that the reader is rendered incapable of escaping from it' as a great writer once said. Far from it. My intention quite simply was to make as much sense as possible of what's taking place all around us by taking into consideration the general mood across the land and by enlarging the frame of reference as much as possible.

2007, OR THE PALACE OF DREAMS

I count myself among those readers who have belatedly come to appreciate the work of the Albanian writer Ismael Kadaré. Having witnessed the wild enthusiasm with which the 1980s literary set embraced the author of *The General of the Dead Army*, I repeatedly postponed an encounter with his opus. Eventually I enjoyed reading *The Palace of Dreams*[67] and became attached to the author's *oeuvre*, even though I in no way share his opinions about the socialist experience in Europe or elsewhere. In any case, in *The Palace of Dreams* the protagonist is appointed to a position in the innermost chambers of the palace's inner circle, at the power structure's very centre. There, he is tasked with collecting, classifying and analysing the dreams of all the kingdom's subjects, gathered from the most far-flung corners of the country and then duly transcribed and recorded by a multitudinous army of official agents and servants, both secret and public.

The authorities' activities, and the manner in which they exert control, entail an incessant back-and-forth movement between the central power structure and the different sites—local, provincial and regional—in which dreams are registered and processed. Because of his skills and his work, but also probably because of his connections—he's a member of the strongman's family—the hero is promoted to the department tasked with the interpretation of dreams, a step up on the hierarchical ladder. The department which handles dreams is the focus of all of the administration's labour, movement, positioning, manoeuvring and modus vivendi as well as of the compromises struck by the novel's political personages.

Ineluctably, the narrative's logic leads the reader to the enigma of the master-dream, the dream of dreams which confers sense to the reality that the regime produces. The novel's denouement entails turbulence in the uppermost echelons, a series of assassinations and the replacement of one strongman for another. For those who'd mastered the art of reading dreams, the cataclysm was legible in the master-dream's entrails. In this oneiric tale, Kadaré doesn't provide the keys to a political interpretation of dreams. He does, however, draw attention to the old problem of the relation between dreaming and the practice of politics.

A few days before the end of 2006, at a little evergreen spot in Old Agdal-Rabat which after all these years I'm still happy to frequent, I found myself chatting with an old friend, a veteran activist in Al Adl Wal Ihssane.[68] I asked him how dreams—both individual and collective—are linked to the work the movement has been doing for years. He replied with boundless assurance that a ceaseless succession of extraordinary events was about to start taking place. He specified that the looming changes would surpass in scale such phenomena as protests, insurrections, uprisings or natural calamities, and that sweeping and transcendent transformations were about to occur. I was so enthralled by the conviction and faith with which my interlocutor evoked his prophecy that I spent the new few days on the lookout for portents of the coming cataclysm. In the end, however, it never came!

Although the year 2007 was meant to culminate with the dream of Sheikh Yassine and his disciples, the dream did not come true in any way whatsoever, at least insofar as I'm aware. The extraordinary and portentous events that had been foretold simply did not come to pass. One can even ask oneself whether any event took place in 2007 that after due consideration could be deemed significant. After all, hadn't the year been a 'lost' one in political, economic and social terms? I think that to nod in assent to this assertion would be to overstate the case, since in fact this was the first true year of the new era, the year of reports, the year of elections, of a new government, of greater regional autonomy, of large-scale construction projects, of the Golden Jubilee festivities, and of much else besides. In other words, although the auguries may have been wide of the mark, the year was indeed significant.

Granada, January 2008

NOTES

1 The first volume of Marcel Proust's seven-volume novel, *À la recherche du temps perdu* (*In Search of Lost Time*), whose narrator is fascinated by Madame de Guermantes.

2 Numidia was the state of the Numidian Amazigh (Berber) peoples, located in present-day Algeria and Tunisia. Founded as an independent state in 202 BCE, it was annexed by the Roman province in 46 BCE, and subsequently became a Roman client-state.

3 Mauretania Tingitana (Latin for 'Tangerine Mauritania') was a province of Rome in North Africa, coinciding roughly with the northern part of present-day Morocco. Its capital city was Tingis (Tamazight: *Tingi*), which occupied the heart of where present-day Tangiers stands.

4 A Rabat-based research institute in the social sciences, focused on Morocco and the Maghreb, and named after Jacques Berque, the French-Algerian anthropologist and sociologist of modern Islam and of the Arab world.

5 A storied art-deco coffee-shop, chocolatier and caterer located in downtown Cairo. Founded by a Swiss immigrant at the turn of the twentieth century, the cafe was emblematic of Egypt's pre–Second World War cosmopolitanism and served as a meeting place for politicians, reformers and writers. It also catered for government functions.

6 Arabic for 'awakening' or 'renaissance'. The Nahda was a cultural movement that began in the late nineteenth and early

twentieth centuries in Egypt, then later spread to other parts of the Arab world. It is often regarded as a period of intellectual modernization and reform, whose effects were felt in religion, literature and language, among other areas.

7 Le Centre d'études et de Recherches en Sciences Sociales is a Rabat-based research institute in the social sciences, founded and directed by Abdallah Saaf. (http://cerss-ma.org)

8 The largest square in Meknes, built in the 1670s by Sultan Moulay Ismaïl between the old city and the new palace he commissioned for himself.

9 A term used in the Maghreb to designate property (usually landed property) that is set aside for charitable ends, according to directives established by Islamic jurisprudence.

10 A term that designates the process of transferring title deeds to assignees and their successors.

11 Also called the Second Moroccan War, the Rif War (1921–26) was fought between the colonial power in the north of Morocco, Spain, later joined by France (which colonized most of the rest of the country), and the Imazighen ('Berbers') of the Rif mountainous region. Led by Abd el-Krim, leader of the Republic of the Rif, which declared independence both from Spain and from the Moroccan Sultanate, the Riffians at first inflicted several defeats on the Spanish forces by using guerrilla tactics and captured European weapons, most notably at the battle of Annual (1921) in which Riffian irregulars killed several thousand Spanish soldiers. Eventually overpowered by the combined forces of Spain and France, the Riffians surrendered and Abd el-Krim was taken into exile.

12 Jean-Paul Charnay (1928–2013), French sociologist at the CNRS (National Centre for Scientific Research) in Paris. A specialist in modern Islam and the Arab World, Charnay spent

his youth in Algeria and frequently collaborated with Jacques Berque.

13 The second largest city in Algeria. Located in the north-west corner of the country, it is much closer to Morocco's eastern border than to the Algerian capital, Algiers.

14 The land border between Morocco and Algeria has been closed since 1994, when Rabat imposed visa regulations on Algerian visitors in the wake of a terrorist attack on the Atlas Asni Hotel in Marrakech in which two Spanish tourists were killed. At the time, the Moroccan government suspected that the Algerian secret service was involved in the bombing. Algeria, for its part, later claimed that Morocco was harbouring Islamist rebels who carried out a 1999 massacre on Algerian soil near the border between the two countries. Another source of contention between the two is that Algeria backs the POLISARIO movement which seeks independence for the Western Sahara, a territory formerly colonized by Spain and annexed by Morocco in 1975.

15 One of several territories along Morocco's Mediterranean coast which are under Spanish rule, Melilla was conquered by Spain in 1497. Like the city of Ceuta, Melilla (pop. around 78,000) is an autonomous city within the Spanish state and both are subject to a sovereignty claim by Morocco. Melilla's population consists largely of ethnic Spaniards and of ethnic Riffian Imazighen, as well as small Sephardic and Sindhi minorities.

16 The term used to describe a period during King Hassan II's reign (mainly the 1960s to the mid-1980s) marked by state violence against left-wing and Islamist dissidents.

17 A sub-region of the Rif, consisting of massifs and plains, the historical home of the Kebdana branch of the Riffian Imazighen.

18 In some Arabic-speaking countries, a *wadi* is the name given to a valley, ravine or channel that is dry except in the rainy season.

19 The period of the Spanish Protectorate in Morocco.

20 A derivative of the cannabis plant widely cultivated throughout the Rif, especially in the zone around Mt Ketama. Its growth, distribution and use has allegedly been tolerated by the authorities as a way of quelling discontent in the north.

21 In late 1958, prompted by widespread unemployment and by a complete lack of representation in the Moroccan central government, an uprising against the Moroccan state took place in the Rif region. In January 1959, Crown Prince Moulay Hassan, who later became King Hassan II, led an army of more than 30,000 soldiers in quelling the revolt. The following month, the Moroccan air force dropped napalm and bombs on rebel hideouts and decisively put an end to the rebellion.

22 A reference to the Chafarinas Islands (in Spanish 'Las Islas Chafarinas'), a trio of islets located close to the Moroccan coast between Nador and Saâïdia that have been in Spanish hands since 1848. Along with a peninsula and a handful of other small islands situated along Morocco's Mediterranean littoral, the Chafarinas are ruled by the central Spanish government, unlike the cities of Ceuta and Melilla which enjoy autonomous status within Spain's system of regional governance.

23 Driss Basri (1938–2007) was a Moroccan politician who, under King Hassan II, served as a hardline minister of the interior from 1979 to 1999. During the Years of Lead, he was commonly associated with the regime's repressive policies towards political dissidents and reformers. In 1999, in a move widely regarded as a sign of the new monarchy's more democratic leanings, Hassan II's son, the newly installed King Mohammed

VI, relieved Basri of his duties. Basri then moved to Paris, where he died in self-imposed exile.

24 The Manhasset negotiations (also known as Manhasset I, II, III and IV) were a series of talks that took place in four rounds in 2007–08 at Manhasset, New York between the Moroccan government and the representatives of the Saharawi independence movement, the POLISARIO Front, to resolve the dispute between both parties over the status of the Western Sahara. In Chapter 14, the author describes his trip to the disputed region.

25 A 1995 novel by Albanian writer Ismail Kadaré. See Saaf's reflection on the relevance to Morocco of a previous novel by Kadaré's in the epilogue, '2007, or *The Palace of Dreams*'.

26 Abdelkebir Khatibi (1938–2009) was a prominent Moroccan sociologist, novelist, playwright and literary and cultural critic.

27 Festivals originally held in honour of holy men and women but these days often also associated with harvest celebrations or with commercial activities.

28 Founded in 1934, Istiqlal is a centre-right nationalist party that played a key role in the struggle for independence and then become the backbone of the legal opposition to the governments of King Hassan II's regime. After Mohammed VI acceded to the throne, Istiqlal became a major party in the new dispensation. In the 2007 elections, it won the largest number of seats and went on to head a coalition government until 2011 when the Islamist Justice and Development Party obtained a victory at the polls.

29 The Moroccan Parliament is comprised of two houses: the House of Representatives and the House of Councilors. The 325 members of the House of Representatives are elected for a five-year term by direct universal suffrage while the members of the former are elected for a six-year term by indirect universal suffrage.

30 A variant of the sirocco winds that blow from the Sahara towards North Africa's coastal zones and beyond.

31 Mohamed El Yazghi (1935–), Moroccan lawyer and politician. Former head of the Union of Socialist Popular Forces (USFP) and minister in various governments.

32 An Arabic daily newspaper headquartered in London.

33 Robert Kagan (1958–) is an American historian, author, columnist and foreign-policy commentator.

34 *Al-Massae* ('The Evening') is an independent Arabic-language Moroccan daily, launched in 2006, while *L'Economiste* is a Casablanca-based francophone daily focusing on economic and financial affairs.

35 A Salafi jihadist militant network of groups based in Morocco and Spain with links to al-Qaeda. Notably responsible for the 2003 Casablanca bombings, a series of coordinated attacks on four different targets, in which twelve suicide bombers killed 33 people and injured over 100.

36 A large cargo and passenger port located in the part of Morocco's Mediterranean coast that's closest to the Iberian Peninsula, between Tangiers and Ceuta, which went into operation in 2007. The port and the free-trade zone attached to it both benefit from their location on the Strait of Gibraltar, one of the world's busiest maritime waterways.

37 In Morocco, *zawiyas* were originally the buildings in which Sufi brotherhoods met. They also served as religious schools and as inns for travellers on religious pilgrimages. Metonymically, the word is sometimes used to designate the brotherhoods themselves.

38 An annual holiday that commemorates the day on which the French colonial authorities sent Sultan Mohammed V into exile because of his sympathy for the independence movement.

39 Skirting Tangiers city centre, the new section of roadway to which the author refers here links the long-established motorway that runs between Rabat and Tangiers along the Atlantic Coast with Tetouan, which is located east of Tangiers and just inland from Morocco's Mediterranean coast. 'Tangiers-Port' refers to the old port inside the Bay of Tangiers. 'Tangiers-Med' refers to the much larger port commissioned by King Mohammed VI and located midway between Tangiers and Tetouan.

40 Spanish for 'pills'.

41 A synthetic drug that can have powerful hallucinatory effects and make the user violent.

42 The Moroccan chapter of L'Association pour la Taxation des Transactions financière et l'Aide aux Citoyens (Association for the Taxation of Financial Transactions and Aid to Citizens), an international grassroots network that opposes neoliberal globalization and works towards social, environmental and democratic alternatives. In Morocco, where a chapter of ATTAC was launched in 2000, the name which the acronym stands for has been partly altered to read L'Association pour la Taxation des Transactions et pour l'Action Citoyenne (Association for Taxation on Transactions and for Citizen Action).

43 One of several epithets by which Marrakech is referred to.

44 The grandson of French settlers, Paul Pascon was born in Fez in 1932 and took Moroccan nationality in the early 1960s. A specialist in the sociology of the Moroccan countryside, Pascon directed an interdisciplinary research unit and wrote a two-volume study of the landholding system of the Haouz region.

45 Earthen channels used in irrigation.

46 Networks of tunnels and wells used on either side of the High Atlas for irrigation and drinking.

47 An Amazigh dynasty originating in the Sahara region which ruled over a large part of what is today Morocco and Spain between 1040 and 1147 CE.

48 A dynasty originating in a different branch of the Amazigh peoples that seized Marrakech, overthrew the Almoravids in 1147 CE and proceeded to build an empire even larger than that of their predecessors, one which at its height included much of present-day Morocco, Algeria, Tunisia, Libya, Western Sahara, Portugal and Spain. Eventually reduced to Marrakech and its environs, the Almohad dominion was taken over in 1269, when the Almohades were conquered by another Amazigh dynasty, the Marinids. The Almohades left a notable architectural legacy, which includes the Giralda Tower of the Cathedral—formerly the Grand Mosque—of Seville, the Hassan Tower in Rabat and the Koutoubia Tower in Marrakech.

49 A dynasty that ruled over Morocco from 1549 to 1659 CE. One of their sultans built the opulent El Badi Palace in Marrakech, the ruins of which are today a popular tourist attraction. Members of the Alaouite Dynasty, which succeeded that of the Saadians, have been Morocco's monarchs ever since.

50 Gueliz and Hivernage are parts of Marrakech that were designed by French colonial town-planners during the Protectorate. Completed in the late twelfth century by the Almohades, the minaret of the Koutoubia mosque is Marrakech's iconic landmark.

51 Of Prophet Muhammad's lineage. The Alaoui dynasty and its predecessors both claim a Sharifian genealogy.

52 An Egyptian economist (1931–), best known for his work on questions of development and underdevelopment and for his critiques of neoliberal globalization.

53 One of a pair of terms used by colonial historians to character-ize the overarching sociopolitical structure of precolonial

Morocco. In this schema, Blad-as Siba was the collective name given to zones of the country (usually the Tamazight-speaking highlands and deserts) which refused to recognize royal author- ity and periodically rebelled against it. Makhzen ('the Treas- ury') was the figure for the latter, and Blad-al-Makhzen was used to refer to those parts of the country (chiefly the Arabic- speaking coastal plains and urban areas) in which the sultanate held undisputed sway. Nowadays, Makhzen is commonly used in Morocco to collectively refer to the Establishment, its insti- tutions, its influence and its power.

54 A working-class district of Casablanca.

55 L'Institut Royal de la Culture Amazigh.

56 An administrative division of the State.

57 The author accepts the Moroccan state's view that the Western Sahara, ruled by Spain between 1884 and 1975, and sovereignty over which is claimed by POLISARIO (the Spanish acronym for Popular Front for the Liberation of Saguía el-Hamra and Río de Oro), is Moroccan by historical right. At present, POLISARIO controls the desert areas of the Western Sahara to the east of a large berm put in place and patrolled by the Moroccan military and Morocco controls the remaining and much larger territory, including its coastal plains and largest towns. The author sometimes uses the words 'Sahara' and 'Saharan' to refer to the disputed territory and sometimes to the desert as such.

58 From the Moroccan State's standpoint, echoed here by the author, the three 'Southern Provinces' which make up the por- tion of the Western Sahara under Moroccan control are an integral part of the Moroccan State. From the standpoint of POLISARIO and its supporters, they constitute Moroccan- occupied territory that must give way to an independent state, referred to as the Sahrawi Arab Democratic Republic. Since

1991, the United Nations has kept a peacekeeping mission in Western Sahara to monitor a ceasefire between both parties. The peace between Morocco and POLISARIO has generally held and the two have engaged in various rounds of talks and informal meetings. However, because of continued disagreement between the parties over core issues, the referendum on the territory's future that was supposed to take place under UN supervision in 1992 has yet to be held. In the meantime, as the author documents in this chapter, the Moroccan government has rapidly fostered the region's socioeconomic development.

59 Jean and Jérôme Tharaud were French brothers who, from 1898 to 1951, co-authored a large number of travel narratives, several of which were based on their travels in Morocco.

60 A dish of slow-cooked lamb, usually roasted on a spit, served on a large platter and traditionally eaten with the hands. It is often served at weddings or other social occasions.

61 Tindouf is a town in Western Algeria, located in an area where the borders of Morocco, Western Sahara and Mauritania are fairly close to one another. During the armed conflict between the Moroccan armed forces and POLISARIO, the front's guerrillas would make forays into the Western Sahara from bases in Tindouf and its environs. At the time of writing (2017), Tindouf continues to host refugee camps for Western Saharans.

62 In French, 'alternance' denotes 'alternation'. In this context, the reference is to the two administrations headed by the veteran socialist politician Abderrahmane el-Youssoufi between 1998 and 2002. The administrations were the outcome of a negotiated settlement with the monarchy that allowed opposition parties to contest the elections and gain ministerial portfolios but that also retained key portfolios in the monarchy's hands. Between September 2000 and September 2002, the author

served as the minister of secondary and technical education in el-Youssoufi's second administration.

63 'The national cause' is here held to mean the complete absorption of Western Sahara into the Moroccan state and, more broadly, Moroccan territorial unity, previously in the face of Spanish and French colonialism, and currently vis-à-vis the independence claims of Saharawi nationalists.

64 In the early 1990s, the implementation of the Schengen Accords and the concomitant reinforcement of Europe's external frontiers led to a notable increase in seaborne clandestine migration across the Strait of Gibraltar. After a new surveillance system went into effect in the strait, migratory routes shifted to an arc of sites along the stretch of coast from Senegal to the Western Sahara. From those sites, migrants travel by boat (usually a motor-powered dugout) across hazardous stretches of the Atlantic to Spain's Canary Islands. In 2006, over 30,000 migrants arrived in the Canaries by boat.

65 The term 'Southern Provinces' designates the southernmost administrative units of the Moroccan state. The provinces, which are grouped in three regional entities, correspond more or less to those parts of the former Spanish Sahara that are under Moroccan control. The provinces are sometimes collectively referred to as 'the South' or as 'the Moroccan Sahara' or as 'Saharan provinces'.

66 The implication of the author's use of the word 'retrocession' is that El-Aiún was formally ceded to Morocco. Its status, however, remains in dispute.

67 First published in Albanian in 1981, *The Palace of Dreams* has appeared in an English translation by Barbara Bray (New York, 1998 and 2011) and in a French translation by Jusuf Vrioni (Paris, 1993), as well as in other languages.

68 A Moroccan Islamist association founded by Sheikh Abdesslam
Yassine whose name translates into 'Justice and Spirituality' or
as 'Justice and Charity'. Although the Moroccan authorities
tolerate the association, it has not been accorded legal status,
in part because it disputes the king's role as 'Commander of
the Faithful'. Under King Hassan II, Sheikh Yassine served
time in prison for his beliefs.